DEPARTMENT OF THE NAVY
HEADQUARTERS UNITED STATES MARINE CORPS
3000 MARINE CORPS PENTAGON
WASHINGTON, DC 20350-3000

I0409696

PRECEDENCE LEVELS FOR MANNING AND STAFFING

DEPARTMENT OF THE NAVY
HEADQUARTERS UNITED STATES MARINE CORPS
3000 MARINE CORPS PENTAGON
WASHINGTON, DC 20350-3000

MCO 5320.12H
C18
4 June 2012

MARINE CORPS ORDER 5320.12H

From: Commandant of the Marine Corps
To: Distribution List

Subj: PRECEDENCE LEVELS FOR MANNING AND STAFFING

Ref: (a) MCO 5311.1D
       (b) MCO M-5210.1

Encl: (1) Excepted Commands
       (2) Operating Forces Commands
       (3) Priority Commands
       (4) Proportionate Share Commands

1. Situation

    a. Budgetary reality determines the need to prioritize and
allocate the total number of personnel, as stated in end
strength terms (not actual inventory), against requirements
(Tables of Organization (T/O)) stated in the Total Force
Structure Management System (TFSMS). This process, known as
"manning," occurs within the Authorized Strength Report (ASR)
and serves as a reflection of how many billets the Marine Corps
can afford to buy. The ASR represents an ideal solution;
results of this process are published semiannually for the
current year, execution year, and the following 19 out-years.

    b. The Deputy Commandant for Manpower and Reserve Affairs
(DC M&RA) manages the current inventory of Marines, builds plans
for the distribution of future inventory, and assigns available,
chargeable inventory against billets "bought" in the ASR process
("staffing"). Frequent changes to structure, policy, cyclical
recruiting trends, training constraints, and unanticipated
personnel losses constrain the inventory available for staffing.
The net effect is that most organizations are staffed with fewer
Marines than prescribed in the unit's T/O or the ASR process.

    c. This Order prioritizes the allocation of planned and
available inventory against T/O requirements. To the maximum
extent possible, every command will be manned by the ASR at the

prescribed precedence level at the Unit Identification Code (UIC) level. Staffing goals will be established by DC M&RA based not only on the precedence levels defined in this Order, but on current inventories and in accordance with other policies that further prioritize the distribution of Marines, such as the Commandant's Planning Guidance when issued to support war time contingencies.

2. <u>Cancellation</u>. MCO 5320.12G.

3. <u>Mission</u>. This Order provides policy for manning and staffing the Marine Corps T/O per reference (a).

4. <u>Execution</u>

   a. <u>Commander's Intent and Concept of Operations</u>

      (1) <u>Commander's Intent</u>. The Marine Corps T/O will be manned and staffed, to the maximum extent possible, per the guidelines established in this Order.

         (a) <u>Manning</u>. Reference (a) establishes the Deputy Commandant for Combat Development and Integration (DC CD&I) as the Total Force Structure Process owner. In this capacity, DC CD&I is responsible for allocating end strength, i.e. manning controls, against the total requirement through the preparation of the ASR reflected in the TFSMS.

         (b) <u>Staffing</u>. Reference (a) further establishes DC M&RA as the Human Resource Development Process owner. In this capacity, DC M&RA is responsible for staffing units based on the priorities established by the Commandant of the Marine Corps (CMC).

         (c) This Order specifies four distinct unit manning precedence level categories, designates the units by UIC that are assigned to these categories, and outlines procedures to change unit manning precedence levels. In addition, CMC establishes minimum manning level "red-lines" for each manning level precedence category.

         (d) This Order establishes that specific billets, or groups of billets, will be "protected" and thus manned at 100 percent, regardless of the billet's parent unit manning precedence level category. Protections are used in cases where within a given UIC there is a specific billet, or billets, which must be manned at 100 percent, however the unit itself is not within the excepted manning precedence level. These protections will be promulgated in the Guidance and ASR Memorandum of Record developed in conjunction with the publication of each ASR.

(2) <u>Concept of Operations</u>

(a) Not all T/O billet requirements will be manned or staffed.

(b) Units will be manned by UIC in accordance with one of the four precedence levels specified in the enclosures. Manning is defined as the portion of a unit's T/O that, within budgetary constraints, is authorized to be filled with Marines. Staffing is defined as the portion of manning that can be filled with assignable inventory in accordance with the priorities established by the CMC.

(c) The current fiscal climate, in concert with the continued operational tempo, has necessitated the need for utmost flexibility and rapid adaptation to evolving manpower conditions. As such, two significant changes have been made to the ASR's methodology in order to respond more quickly and accurately to the Marine Corps' developing manpower needs. The first change is the development of a fourth manning precedence level category, Operating Forces (OpFor), to further differentiate the gradation of precedence levels. The second change is the application of CMC minimum manning level "red-lines." A "red line" describes the minimum aggregate manning of particular UICs, based on that UIC's manning precedence level category. "Red line" manning percentage is derived from the cumulative manning of all manned (or ASR-bought) billets within a particular UIC, to include protected billets. Furthermore, the aggregate manning level of all UICs within a specific manning precedence category should coincide with the minimum "red line" value of that precedence category. The manning and staffing precedence levels and CMC minimum manning level "red-lines" for each manning precedence category are explained below.

<u>1</u>. <u>Excepted Command</u>. Excepted commands are those commands that fill a vital or mandated need. The CMC minimum manning level "red-line" is established at 100 percent for both officers and enlisted Marines within the Excepted manning precedence level category, subject to inventory availability.

<u>2</u>. <u>OpFor Command</u>. OpFor commands are those commands that have been identified as integral to current

3

operational needs. They will be manned at a percentage of chargeable T/O by grade and Military Occupational Specialty (MOS) that will best meet the operational tempo while still supporting other competing needs of the Marine Corps. The CMC minimum manning level "red-line" is 95 percent for officers and 97 percent for enlisted Marines within the OpFor manning precedence level category, subject to inventory availability.

3. <u>Priority Command</u>. Priority commands are those commands that while not excepted or specifically integral to the operating forces, serve a significant function. As such, Priority commands shall be manned in accordance with prevailing manning conditions of chargeable T/O by grade and MOS. The CMC minimum manning level "red-line" is 95 percent for both officers and enlisted Marines within the Priority manning precedence level category, subject to inventory availability.

4. <u>Proportionate Share Command (Pro-Share)</u>. Pro-Share commands are those units not categorized within the Excepted, OpFor or Priority manning precedence levels. Pro-Share commands will be manned at a percentage of chargeable T/O by grade and MOS. The CMC minimum manning level "red-line" is 92 percent for officers and 94 percent for enlisted Marines within the Pro-Share manning precedence level category, subject to inventory availability.

5. <u>Joint Duty Assignment List (JDAL)</u>. Manning and staffing levels for JDAL billets will be established via the Commandant's Planning Guidance and further elaborated in the ASR Guidance and Memorandum of Record developed in conjunction with the publication of each ASR.

6. <u>Marine Forces Reserve (MARFORRES)</u>. MARFORRES units will be categorized under the same four manning and staffing precedence levels described in this Order. However, since each MARFORRES unit can have up to three different types of manpower resources (Active Duty in Support of Reserves (ADSR), Selected Marine Corps Reserve (SMCR), and Active Reserves (AR)), the manning of individual billets will either coincide with the UIC's precedence category or be manned at 100 percent as a protected billet(s). Regardless of the presence of protections, the aggregate manning level of a particular MARFORRES UIC will coincide with its prescribed manning precedence category described in this Order, and meet or exceed the CMC's "red lines."

4

b. Coordinating Instructions

(1) In the event that the assignable inventory is inadequate to meet the T/O requirement, grade and MOS substitution may be used to facilitate the staffing of billets. Grade and MOS substitution will be kept to a minimum.

(2) The broad intent of this Order is to prioritize manning and staffing levels. However, combat or contingency operations and commitments require that CMC retain the flexibility to deviate from the established precedence levels, with emphasis on institutional preservation and contingency warfighting requirements. The CMC is the sole decision making authority for adjusting unit manning and staffing levels outside of the levels established by this Order.

(3) The enclosures list all existent and planned units by UIC within TFSMS during the Future Years Defense Plan (FYDP), Fiscal Years (FY) 12-18. The UICs beginning with the letter "M" denote units already in existence in FY12. UICs beginning with the letter "P" identify the units not currently in existence, but are planned for phasing into existence at some point during the FYDP.

(4) Enclosure (1) lists commands to be manned and staffed at the Excepted manning precedence level. Enclosure (2) lists commands to be manned and staffed at the OpFor manning precedence level. Enclosure (3) lists commands to be manned and staffed at the Priority manning precedence level. Enclosure (4) lists commands to be manned and staffed at the Pro-Share manning precedence level category.

(5) Recommended changes to the enclosures will be submitted to DC CD&I (Total Force Structure Division) for analysis and staffing to the MARFORs, Advocates, M&RA, and CMC for approval. Changes will be considered every four years, normally within six months of the ascension of a new Commandant or as directed by CMC to accommodate manning and staffing requirements in support of dynamic operational demands. Change requests must be signed at the 3-star general officer level and will include the following information.

(a) The purpose and justification of the change request.

(b) The operational impact of the change request.

(c) The UIC(s) the change request affects.

(d) The current and proposed precedence level(s).

5. Administration and Logistics

a. This Order contains content and administrative changes. Individuals assigned to Headquarters Marine Corps staff agencies, field commanders, and other persons concerned with the manning and staffing precedence process must review the entire Order to become familiar with the new policies in effect.

b. Records created as a result of this directive shall include records management requirements to ensure the proper maintenance and use of records, regardless of format or medium, to promote accessibility and authorized retention per the approved records schedule and reference (b).

6. Command and Signal

a. Command. This Order is applicable to the Marine Corps Total Force based on the manning and staffing precedence in paragraph 4a(2)(c) of this Order.

b. Signal. This Order is effective the date signed.

JAMES F. AMOS

DISTRIBUTION: PCN 10207900600

Copy to: 7000260/8145005 (2)
7000099/8145001 (1)

Excepted Commands

UIC	UNIT NAME	MAGTF
MS4307	HMX-1 EXEC SPT MCAF QUANTICO VA	ACE
M30605	CE MARFOR CYBERCOM	CE
M30008	MARCOR AUGMTN & TRNG SPT UNIT MARFORSOC	CE
M53530	MCSF BN BANGOR MCSF REGT	CE
M53520	MCSF BN KINGS BAY MCSF REGT	CE
MS5607	12TH MARINE CORPS DISTRICT HQTRS	SE
MS5602	1ST MARINE CORPS DISTRICT HQTRS	SE
MS5603	4TH MARINE CORPS DISTRICT HQTRS	SE
MS5604	6TH MARINE CORPS DISTRICT HQTRS	SE
MS5605	8TH MARINE CORPS DISTRICT HQTRS	SE
MS5606	9TH MARINE CORPS DISTRICT HQTRS	SE
MS3003	MC AFGANPAK HANDS	SE
MS4202	US MILITARY ENLISTMENT PROCESSING CENTER (MEPCOM)	SE

Operating Forces Commands

*Denotes the geographic movement and name change of these units during the FYDP.

UIC	UNIT NAME	MAGTF
M00102	HQTRS 1ST MAW	ACE
M00203	HQTRS 2D MAW	ACE
M00319	HQTRS 3D MAW	ACE
M01129	HQTRS 4TH MAW	ACE
M00923	FIRING BTRY A 2D LAAD BN MACG-28 2D MAW	ACE
M00933	FIRING BTRY A 3D LAAD BN MACG-38 3D MAW	ACE
M00924	FIRING BTRY B 2D LAAD BN MACG-28 2D MAW	ACE
M00934	FIRING BTRY B 3D LAAD BN MACG-38 3D MAW	ACE
M00920	HQTRS 2D LAAD BN MACG-28 2D MAW	ACE
M00931	HQTRS 3D LAAD BN MACG-38 3D MAW	ACE
M00921	H&S BTRY 2D LAAD BN MACG-28 2D MAW	ACE
M00935	H&S BTRY 3D LAAD BN MACG-38 3D MAW	ACE
M00922	DET H&S BTRY 2D LAAD BN MACG-28 2D MAW	ACE
M00932	DET H&S BTRY 3D LAAD BN MACG-38 3D MAW	ACE
M01152	VMGR-152 MAG-36 1ST MAW	ACE
M01234	VMGR-234 MAG-41 4TH MAW	ACE
M01252	VMGR-252 MAG-14 2D MAW	ACE
M01352	VMGR-352 MAG-11 3D MAW	ACE
M01233	VMGR-452 MAG-49 4TH MAW	ACE
M01130	VMFA-112 MAG-41 4TH MAW	ACE
M01115	VMFA-115 MAG-31 2D MAW	ACE
M01122	VMFA-122 MAG-31 2D MAW	ACE
M01232	VMFA-232 MAG-11 3D MAW	ACE
M01251	VMFA-251 MAG-31 2D MAW	ACE
M01312	VMFA-312 MAG-31 2D MAW	ACE
M01314	VMFA-314 MAG-11 3D MAW	ACE
M01323	VMFA-323 MAG-11 3D MAW	ACE
M01192	VMFAT-101 MAG-11 3D MAW	ACE
M09934	VMFAT-501 MAG-31 2D MAW	ACE
M01194	VMFAT-502 MAG 31 2D MAW	ACE
M01121	VMFA (AW)-121 MAG-11 3D MAW	ACE
M01224	VMFA (AW)-224 MAG-31 2D MAW	ACE
M01225	VMFA (AW)-225 MAG-11 3D MAW	ACE
M01242	VMFA (AW)-242 MAG-12 1ST MAW	ACE
M01533	VMFA (AW)-533 MAG-31 2D MAW	ACE
M06332	VMFA-332 MAG-13 3D MAW (16 Plane)	ACE
P01115	VMFA-115 MAG-31 2D MAW (10 Plane)	ACE
P01211	VMFA-211 MAG-13 3D MAW (10 Plane)	ACE
M05212	VMFA-212 MAG-13 3D MAW (10 Plane)	ACE
P01224	VMFA-224 MAG-31 2D MAW (10 Plane)	ACE
M05332	VMFA-332 MAG-13 3D MAW (10 Plane)	ACE
M01211	VMA-211 MAG-13 3D MAW	ACE
M01214	VMA-214 MAG-13 3D MAW	ACE
M01223	VMA-223 MAG-14 2D MAW	ACE

M01231	VMA-231 MAG-14 2D MAW	ACE
M01311	VMA-311 MAG-13 3D MAW	ACE
M01513	VMA-513 MAG-13 3D MAW	ACE
M01542	VMA-542 MAG-14 2D MAW	ACE
M01362	HMH-362 MAG-24 (-) 1ST MAW	ACE
M01363	HMH-363 MAG-24 (-) 1ST MAW	ACE
M01361	HMH-361 MAG-16 3D MAW	ACE
M01366	HMH-366 MAG-29 2D MAW	ACE
M01461	HMH-461 MAG-29 2D MAW	ACE
M01462	HMH-462 MAG-16 3D MAW	ACE
P01463	HMH-463 MAG-24(-) 1ST MAW	ACE
M01464	HMH-464 MAG-29 2D MAW	ACE
M01465	HMH-465 MAG-16 3D MAW	ACE
M01466	HMH-466 MAG-16 3D MAW	ACE
M01772	HMH-772 (-) MAG-49 4TH MAW	ACE
M05161	VMM-161 MAG-16 3D MAW	ACE
M05162	VMM-162 MAG-26 2D MAW	ACE
M05163	VMM-163 MAG-16 3D MAW	ACE
M05164	VMM-164 MAG-39 3D MAW	ACE
M05165	VMM-165 MAG-16 3D MAW	ACE
M05166	VMM-166 MAG-16 3D MAW	ACE
M05261	VMM-261 MAG-26 2D MAW	ACE
M05262	VMM-262 MAG-36 1ST MAW	ACE
M05263	VMM-263 MAG-26 2D MAW	ACE
M05264	VMM-264 MAG-26 2D MAW	ACE
M05265	VMM-265 MAG-36 1ST MAW	ACE
M05266	VMM-266 MAG-26 2D MAW	ACE
M05268	VMM-268 MAG-39 3D MAW	ACE
M05363	VMM-363 MAG-24(-) 1ST MAW	ACE
M05364	VMM-364 MAG-39 3D MAW	ACE
M05365	VMM-365 MAG-26 2D MAW	ACE
M04801	DET VMR ANDREWS AFB 4TH MAW	ACE
M03017	DET VMR BELLE CHASSE 4TH MAW	ACE
M01262	HMM-262 MAG-36 1ST MAW	ACE
M01265	HMM-265 MAG-36 1ST MAW	ACE
M01268	HMM-268 MAG-39 3D MAW	ACE
M01364	HMM-364 MAG-39 3D MAW	ACE
M01764	HMM-764 MAG-41 4TH MAW	ACE
M01774	HMM-774 MAG-49 4TH MAW	ACE
M01169	HMLA-167 MAG-29 2D MAW	ACE
M01173	HMLA-169 MAG-39 3D MAW	ACE
M01267	HMLA-267 MAG-39 3D MAW	ACE
M01269	HMLA-269 MAG-29 2D MAW	ACE
M01367	HMLA-367 MAG-39 3D MAW	ACE
M01369	HMLA-369 MAG-39 3D MAW	ACE
M01470	HMLA-467 MAG-29 2D MAW	ACE
M01469	HMLA-469 MAG-39 3D MAW	ACE
M01773	HMLA-773 MAG-49 4TH MAW	ACE
M01237	VMAQ-1 MAG-14 2D MAW	ACE

M01238	VMAQ-2 MAG-14 2D MAW	ACE
M01239	VMAQ-3 MAG-14 2D MAW	ACE
M01010	VMAQ-4 MAG-14 2D MAW	ACE
M00328	MAWTS-1 TECOM MCAS YUMA AZ	ACE
M01181	HMHT-302 MAG-29 2D MAW	ACE
M01195	HMLAT-303 MAG-39 3D MAW	ACE
M01175	HMMT-164 MAG-39 3D MAW	ACE
M01171	VMMT-204 MAG-26 2D MAW	ACE
M04161	MATSG-42 TRNG COM NAS PENSACOLA FL	ACE
M09933	VMFT-401 MCAS YUMA AZ	ACE
M01203	VMAT-203 MAG-14 2D MAW	ACE
M00111	MARINE AVN AIRCREW TRNG SYSTEM HQTRS 1ST MAW	ACE
M00218	MARINE AVN AIRCREW TRNG SYSTEM HQTRS 2D MAW	ACE
M00334	MARINE AVN AIRCREW TRNG SYSTEM HQTRS 3D MAW	ACE
M00893	MARINE AVN AIRCREW TRNG SYSTEM HQTRS 4TH MAW	ACE
M00105	3D SP SEC COMM TM HQTRS 1ST MAW	ACE
M00326	4TH SP SEC COMM TM HQTRS 3D MAW	ACE
M00208	6TH SP SEC COMM TM HQTRS 2D MAW	ACE
M00618	HQTRS MACG-18 1ST MAW	ACE
M00628	HQTRS MACG-28 2D MAW	ACE
M00638	HQTRS MACG-38 3D MAW	ACE
M00648	HQTRS MACG-48 4TH MAW	ACE
M00885	HQTRS MACS-1 MACG-38 3D MAW	ACE
M00871	HQTRS MACS-2 MACG-28 2D MAW	ACE
M01308	HQTRS MACS-23 MACG-48 4TH MAW	ACE
M01309	HQTRS MACS-24 MACG-48 4TH MAW	ACE
M00861	HQTRS MACS-4 MACG-18 1ST MAW	ACE
M00881	DET TAOC MACS-1 MACG-38 3D MAW	ACE
M00872	DET TAOC MACS-2 MACG-28 2D MAW	ACE
M01341	DET TAOC MACS-23 MACG-48 4TH MAW	ACE
M01235	DET TAOC MACS-24 MACG-48 4TH MAW	ACE
M00862	DET TAOC MACS-4 MACG-18 1ST MAW	ACE
M00886	DET EW/C MACS-1 MACG-38 3D MAW	ACE
M00873	DET EW/C MACS-2 MACG-28 2D MAW	ACE
M01335	DET EW/C MACS-23 MACG-48 4TH MAW	ACE
M00882	DET A ATC MACS-1 MACG-38 3D MAW	ACE
M00874	DET A ATC MACS-2 MACG-28 2D MAW	ACE
M01236	DET A ATC MACS-24 MACG-48 4TH MAW	ACE
M00863	DET A ATC MACS-4 MACG-18 1ST MAW	ACE
M00883	DET B ATC MACS-1 MACG-38 3D MAW	ACE
M00875	DET B ATC MACS-2 MACG-28 2D MAW	ACE
M00864	DET B ATC MACS-4 MACG-18 1ST MAW	ACE
M00884	DET C ATC MACS-1 MACG-38 3D MAW	ACE
M00876	DET C ATC MACS-2 MACG-28 2D MAW	ACE
M01143	MTACS-18 MACG-18 1ST MAW	ACE
M01145	MTACS-28 MACG-28 2D MAW	ACE
M01144	MTACS-38 MACG-38 3D MAW	ACE
M01146	MTACS-48 MACG-48 4TH MAW	ACE
M00891	AVN CMD AND CTRL TM 4TH MAW	ACE

Enclosure (2)

M00820	MASS-1 MACG-28 2D MAW	ACE
M00825	MASS-2 MACG-18 1ST MAW	ACE
M00830	MASS-3 MACG-38 3D MAW	ACE
M00983	MASS-6 MACG-48 4TH MAW	ACE
M03028	MASS-6 (FWD) MACG-48 4TH MAW	ACE
M01215	EA-6 SPT MAG-12 1ST MAW	ACE
M01027	MWHS-1 HQTRS 1ST MAW	ACE
M01053	MWHS-2 HQTRS 2D MAW	ACE
M01079	MWHS-3 HQTRS 3D MAW	ACE
M00109	HQTRS MWCS-18 MACG-18 1ST MAW	ACE
M00212	HQTRS MWCS-28 MACG-28 2D MAW	ACE
M00310	HQTRS MWCS-38 MACG-38 3D MAW	ACE
M00407	HQTRS MWCS-48 MACG-48 4TH MAW	ACE
M00108	DET A MWCS-18 MACG-18 1ST MAW	ACE
M00210	DET A MWCS-28 MACG-28 2D MAW	ACE
M00308	DET A MWCS-38 MACG-38 3D MAW	ACE
M00409	DET A MWCS-48 (FWD) MACG-48 4TH MAW	ACE
M00408	DET A MWCS-48 (REAR) MACG-48 4TH MAW	ACE
M00209	DET B MWCS-28 MACG-28 2D MAW	ACE
M00309	DET B MWCS-38 MACG-38 3D MAW	ACE
M00133	HQTRS MWSG-47 4TH MAW	ACE
M00510	DET A MWSS-471 MWSG-47 4TH MAW	ACE
M01139	DET A MWSS-473 MWSG-47 4TH MAW	ACE
M00544	DET B MWSS-471 MWSG-47 4TH MAW	ACE
M00542	DET B MWSS-473 MWSG-47 4TH MAW	ACE
M00526	DET A MWSS-472 MWSG-47 4TH MAW	ACE
M00527	DET B MWSS-472 MWSG-47 4TH MAW	ACE
M05171	MWSS-171 MAG-12 1ST MAW	ACE
M05172	MWSS-172 MAG-36 1ST MAW	ACE
M05271	MWSS-271 MAG-14 2D MAW	ACE
M05272	MWSS-272 MAG-26 2D MAW	ACE
M05273	MWSS-273 MAG-31 2D MAW	ACE
M05274	MWSS-274 MAG-29 2D MAW	ACE
M05371	MWSS-371 MAG-13 3D MAW	ACE
M05372	MWSS-372 MAG-39 3D MAW	ACE
M05373	MWSS-373 MAG-11 3D MAW	ACE
M05374	MWSS-374 MAG-16 3D MAW	ACE
M00541	MWSS-471 MWSG-47 4TH MAW	ACE
M00524	MWSS-472 MWSG-47 4TH MAW	ACE
M01149	MWSS-473 MWSG-47 4TH MAW	ACE
M04171	MWSD MAG-24 (-) 1ST MAW	ACE
M00106	CALIB LAB HQTRS 1ST MAW	ACE
M00211	CALIB LAB HQTRS 2D MAW	ACE
M00327	CALIB LAB HQTRS 3D MAW	ACE
M00230	HQTRS MAG-11 3D MAW	ACE
M00237	HQTRS MAG-12 1ST MAW	ACE
M00231	HQTRS MAG-13 3D MAW	ACE
M00214	HQTRS MAG-14 2D MAW	ACE
M00226	HQTRS MAG-26 2D MAW	ACE

M00241	HQTRS MAG-31 2D MAW	ACE
M00242	HQTRS MAG-41 4TH MAW	ACE
M01065	MALS-11 MAG-11 3D MAW	ACE
M01038	MALS-12 MAG-12 1ST MAW	ACE
M01013	MALS-13 MAG-13 3D MAW	ACE
M01068	MALS-14 MAG-14 2D MAW	ACE
M01074	MALS-26 MAG-26 2D MAW	ACE
M01086	MALS-31 MAG-31 2D MAW	ACE
M01136	MALS-41 MAG-41 4TH MAW	ACE
M01193	FDR MALS-11 MAG-11 3D MAW	ACE
M01216	FDR MALS-12 MAG-12 1ST MAW	ACE
M01514	FDR MALS-13 MAG-13 3D MAW	ACE
M01249	FDR MALS-14 MAG-14 2D MAW	ACE
M01174	FDR MALS-26 MAG-26 2D MAW	ACE
M01087	FDR MALS-31 MAG-31 2D MAW	ACE
M01137	FDR MALS-41 MAG-41 4TH MAW	ACE
M01468	FDR MALS-16 MAG-16 3D MAW	ACE
M01467	FDR MALS-24 (-) MAG-24 (-) 1ST MAW	ACE
M01371	FDR MALS-29 MAG-29 2D MAW	ACE
M01270	FDR MALS-36 MAG-36 1ST MAW	ACE
M01198	FDR MALS-39 MAG-39 3D MAW	ACE
M00232	HQTRS MAG-16 3D MAW	ACE
M00229	HQTRS MAG-29 2D MAW	ACE
M00236	HQTRS MAG-36 1ST MAW	ACE
M00233	HQTRS MAG-39 3D MAW	ACE
M00245	HQTRS MAG-49 4TH MAW	ACE
M00234	HQTRS MAG-24 (-) 1ST MAW	ACE
M01020	MALS-16 MAG-16 3D MAW	ACE
M01227	MALS-29 MAG-29 2D MAW	ACE
M01024	MALS-36 MAG-36 1ST MAW	ACE
M01158	MALS-39 MAG-39 3D MAW	ACE
M01197	MALS-49 MAG-49 4TH MAW	ACE
M01071	MALS-24 (-) MAG-24 (-) 1ST MAW	ACE
M00213	2D MAW BAND HQTRS 2D MAW	ACE
M00320	3D MAW BAND HQTRS 3D MAW	ACE
M01480	VMU-1 MACG-38 3D MAW	ACE
M01490	VMU-2 MACG-28 2D MAW	ACE
M01495	VMU-3 MACG-38 3D MAW	ACE
M01485	VMU-4 MACG-48 4TH MAW	ACE
MS0348	DET MARINE SUPT VFA-101 EGLIN AFB	ACE
M03008	SITE SPT (AURORA) MACG-48 4TH MAW	ACE
M03018	SITE SPT (BELLE CHASSE) MAG-49 4TH MAW	ACE
M03021	SITE SPT (EDWARDS AFB) MAG-41 4TH MAW	ACE
M03040	SITE SPT (FRESNO) MWSG-47 4TH MAW	ACE
M03022	SITE SPT (FT HOOD) MACG-48 MARFORRES	ACE
M03007	SITE SPT (FT WORTH) MAG-41 4TH MAW	ACE
M03009	SITE SPT (GREAT LAKES) MACG-48 4TH MAW	ACE
M03045	SITE SPT (JOHNSTOWN) MAG-49 4TH MAW	ACE
M03026	SITE SPT (MCGUIRE AFB) MAG-49 4TH MAW	ACE

M03016	SITE SPT (MINNEAPOLIS) MWSG-47 4TH MAW	ACE
M03027	SITE SPT (MIRAMAR) 4TH MAW	ACE
M03020	SITE SPT (NORFOLK) MAG-49 4TH MAW	ACE
M03044	SITE SPT (OCEANA) MACG-48 4TH MAW	ACE
M03010	SITE SPT (SELFRIDGE) MWSG-47 4TH MAW	ACE
M03042	SITE SPT (STEWART) MAG-49 4TH MAW	ACE
M03004	SITE SPT (WARNER ROBINS AFB) MAG-49 4TH MAW	ACE
M03025	SITE SPT (WESTOVER AFB) MWSG-47 4TH MAW	ACE
M03035	SITE SPT (WYOMING) MWSG-47 4TH MAW	ACE
M03046	SITE SPT (YUMA) MACG-48 4TH MAW	ACE
M00216	ACFT OP TEST & EVAL SUPPORT	ACE
MS0341	CNATT NAS PENSACOLA FL	ACE
MS0340	CNATTU TRNG COM NAS PENSACOLA FL	ACE
MS9935	CNRF COM NORFOLK	ACE
M01778	DET A HMLA-773 MAG-49 4TH MAW	ACE
M01767	DET B HMLA-773 MAG-49 4TH MAW	ACE
MS1196	DET CNATT MCAS CAMPEN CA	ACE
MS0344	DET CNATT MCAS CHERRY POINT NC	ACE
MS1172	DET CNATT MCAS NEW RIVER NC	ACE
MS0330	DET CNATT NAS WHIDBEY ISL WA	ACE
MS0331	DET MARINE SPT VFA-122 NAS LEMOORE CA	ACE
M01488	DET VMU-4 MACG-48 4TH MAW	ACE
MS0329	NAV FTR WPNS SCOL NAS FALLON NV	ACE
MS0342	VFA-106 NAS OCEANA VA	ACE
M01380	VMX-22 MCAS NEW RIVER NC	ACE
M20982	ENGR CO LOG BN MSOSG MARFORSOC	CE
M21571	1ST RAD BN I MEF	CE
M21591	2D RAD BN II MEF	CE
M21541	3D RAD BN III MEF	CE
M21636	HQTRS CO 7TH COMM BN III MEF	CE
M21641	HQTRS CO 8TH COMM BN II MEF	CE
M21672	HQTRS CO 9TH COMM BN I MEF	CE
M20161	CE 11TH MEU I MEF	CE
M20173	CE 13TH MEU I MEF	CE
M20310	CE 15TH MEU I MEF	CE
M18032	CE 22D MEU II MEF	CE
M18045	CE 24TH MEU II MEF	CE
M18038	CE 26TH MEU II MEF	CE
M20175	CE 31ST MEU III MEF	CE
M21634	DS COMM CO A 7TH COMM BN III MEF	CE
M21644	DS COMM CO A 8TH COMM BN II MEF	CE
M21675	DS COMM CO A 9TH COMM BN I MEF	CE
M21645	DS COMM CO B 8TH COMM BN II MEF	CE
M21676	DS COMM CO B 9TH COMM BN I MEF	CE
M21646	DS COMM CO C 8TH COMM BN II MEF	CE
M21677	DS COMM CO C 9TH COMM BN I MEF	CE
M21638	GS COMM CO 7TH COMM BN III MEF	CE
M21643	GS COMM CO 8TH COMM BN II MEF	CE
M21674	GS COMM CO 9TH COMM BN I MEF	CE

Enclosure (2)

M21637	SVC CO 7TH COMM BN III MEF	CE
M21642	SVC CO 8TH COMM BN II MEF	CE
M21673	SVC CO 9TH COMM BN I MEF	CE
M20981	COMM CO CMBT SPT BN MSOSG MARFORSOC	CE
M20911	HQTRS MAR SPEC OPS SCOL MARFORSOC	CE
M20922	DET W MAR SPEC OPS SPT GRP MARFORSOC	CE
M20923	MAR SPEC OPS CO A 1ST MAR SPEC OPS BN MSOR	CE
M20924	MAR SPEC OPS CO B 1ST MAR SPEC OPS BN MSOR	CE
M20925	MAR SPEC OPS CO C 1ST MAR SPEC OPS BN MSOR	CE
M20926	MAR SPEC OPS CO D 1ST MAR SPEC OPS BN MSOR	CE
M20934	MAR SPEC OPS CO F 2D MAR SPEC OPS BN MSOR	CE
M20935	MAR SPEC OPS CO G 2D MAR SPEC OPS BN MSOR	CE
M20936	MAR SPEC OPS CO H 2D MAR SPEC OPS BN MSOR	CE
M20937	MAR SPEC OPS CO I 2D MAR SPEC OPS BN MSOR	CE
M20938	MAR SPEC OPS CO K 3D MAR SPEC OPS BN MSOR	CE
M20952	MAR SPEC OPS CO L 3D MAR SPEC OPS BN MSOR	CE
M20953	MAR SPEC OPS CO M 3D MAR SPEC OPS BN MSOR	CE
M20954	MAR SPEC OPS CO N 3D MAR SPEC OPS BN MSOR	CE
M20941	HQTRS MAR SPEC OPS REGT MARFORSOC	CE
M20971	HQTRS MSOSG MARFORSOC	CE
M20972*	HQTRS CO SPT BN MSOSG MARFORSOC	CE
M20972*	SPT CO MSOSG MARFORSOC	CE
M20973*	HQTRS CO CMBT SPT BN MSOSG MARFORSOC	CE
M20973*	INTEL BN MSOSG MARFORSOC	CE
M20974*	LOG CO MSOSG MARFORSOC	CE
M20974*	HQTRS CO LOG BN MSOSG MARFORSOC	CE
M20976	LOG CO A LOG BN MSOSG MARFORSOC	CE
M20977	LOG CO B LOG BN MSOSG MARFORSOC	CE
M20978	LOG CO C LOG BN MSOSG MARFORSOC	CE
M20921	HQTRS 1ST MAR SPEC OPS BN MSOR	CE
M20931	HQTRS 2D MAR SPEC OPS BN MSOR	CE
M20951	HQTRS 3D MAR SPEC OPS BN MSOR	CE
M21610	1ST ANGLICO MHG I MEF	CE
M21625	2D ANGLICO MHG II MEF	CE
M21626	3D ANGLICO MARFORRES	CE
M21630	4TH ANGLICO MARFORRES	CE
M21631	5TH ANGLICO MHG III MEF	CE
M20364	CBIRF II MEF	CE
M20146	CE I MEF	CE
M20133	CE II MEF	CE
M20129	CE III MEF	CE
M20371	CE MHG I MEF	CE
M20360	CE MHG II MEF	CE
M20381	CE MHG III MEF	CE
M20004	H&S BN MARFORCOM	CE
M20021	H&S BN MARFORPAC	CE
M20001	HQTRS MARFORCOM	CE
M20022	HQTRS MARFORPAC	CE
M20901	HQTRS MARFORSOC	CE

Enclosure (2)

M18511	CE 1ST MEB I MEF	CE
M18521	CE 2D MEB II MEF	CE
M18531	CE 3D MEB III MEF	CE
M20411	CE MEB MARFOR AFRICOM	CE
M20400	MARFOR AFRICOM	CE
M20500	MARFOR CENTCOM	CE
M20600	MARFOR EUCOM	CE
M20800	MARFOR KOREA	CE
M20050	MARFOR NORTHCOM	CE
M20002	MARFOR SOUTHCOM	CE
M20700	MARFOR STRATCOM	CE
P20510	CE MARFOR CENTCOM (FWD)	CE
M20177	III MEF BAND MHG III MEF	CE
M20025	MARFORPAC BAND	CE
M09932	MARINE FORCES RESERVE BAND	CE
M20734	1ST INTEL BN I MEF	CE
M20366	2D INTEL BN II MEF	CE
M20738	3D INTEL BN III MEF	CE
M20735	HQTRS CO 1ST INTEL BN I MEF	CE
M20367	HQTRS CO 2D INTEL BN II MEF	CE
M20739	HQTRS CO 3D INTEL BN III MEF	CE
M20736	PROD & ANALYS CO 1ST INTEL BN I MEF	CE
M20368	PROD & ANALYS CO 2D INTEL BN II MEF	CE
M20782	PROD & ANALYS CO 3D INTEL BN III MEF	CE
M20737	CI/ HUMINT CO 1ST INTEL BN I MEF	CE
M20369	CI/ HUMINT CO 2D INTEL BN II MEF	CE
M20783	CI/ HUMINT CO 3D INTEL BN III MEF	CE
M73010	3D FORECON CO 4TH MARDIV	CE
M28352	4TH FORECON CO (-) 4TH MARDIV	CE
M14717	DET 4TH FORECON CO 4TH MARDIV	CE
M14805	HUMINT EXPLOIT PLT CO A ISB HQTRS MARFORRES	CE
M14828	HUMINT EXPLOIT PLT CO C ISB HQTRS MARFORRES	CE
M14800	INTEL SPT BN MARFORRES	CE
M14803	HQTRS CO A ISB MARFORRES	CE
M14810	HQTRS CO B ISB MARFORRES	CE
M14818	HQTRS CO C ISB MARFORRES	CE
M14802	HQTRS CO 4TH GS PLT ISB MARFORRES	CE
M14807	INTEL PROD TM 1 CO A ISB MARFORRES	CE
M14815	INTEL PROD TM 1 CO B ISB MARFORRES	CE
M14824	INTEL PROD TM 1 CO C ISB MARFORRES	CE
M14808	INTEL PROD TM 2 CO A ISB MARFORRES	CE
M14816	INTEL PROD TM 2 CO B ISB MARFORRES	CE
M14827	INTEL PROD TM 2 CO C ISB MARFORRES	CE
M14809	INTEL PROD TM 3 CO A ISB MARFORRES	CE
M14817	INTEL PROD TM 3 CO B ISB MARFORRES	CE
M14826	INTEL PROD TM 3 CO C ISB MARFORRES	CE
M14804	CI PLT CO A ISB HQTRS MARFORRES	CE
M14819	CI PLT CO C ISB HQTRS MARFORRES	CE
M14806	INTEL AFP CO A ISB MARFORRES	CE

M14814	INTEL AFP CO B ISB MARFORRES	CE
M14823	INTEL AFP CO C ISB MARFORRES	CE
M14811	INTEL IIP CO B ISB MARFORRES	CE
M14812	HST 1 CO B ISB HQTRS MARFORRES	CE
M14821	HST 1 CO C ISB HQTRS MARFORRES	CE
M14813	HST 2 CO B ISB HQTRS MARFORRES	CE
M14822	HST 2 CO C ISB HQTRS MARFORRES	CE
M20733	CI/HUMINT SPT CO 1ST INTEL BN I MEF	CE
M20787	CI/HUMINT SPT CO 2D INTEL BN II MEF	CE
M20732	PROD & ANALYS SPT CO 1ST INTEL BN I MEF	CE
M20786	PROD & ANALYS SPT CO 2D INTEL BN II MEF	CE
M20986	INTEL CO A CMBT SPT BN MSOSG MARFORSOC	CE
M20987	INTEL CO B CMBT SPT BN MSOSG MARFORSOC	CE
M20988	INTEL CO C CMBT SPT BN MSOSG MARFORSOC	CE
M20152	MP CO A LAW ENF BN I MHG I MEF	CE
M20252	MP CO A LAW ENF BN II MHG II MEF	CE
M20352	MP CO A LAW ENF BN III MHG III MEF	CE
M20153	MP CO B LAW ENF BN I MHG I MEF	CE
M20253	MP CO B LAW ENF BN II MHG II MEF	CE
M20353	MP CO B LAW ENF BN III MHG III MEF	CE
M20154	MP CO C LAW ENF BN I MHG I MEF	CE
M20254	MP CO C LAW ENF BN II MHG II MEF	CE
M20354	MP CO C LAW ENF BN III MHG III MEF	CE
M20151	HQTRS CO LAW ENF BN I MHG I MEF	CE
M20251	HQTRS CO LAW ENF BN II MHG II MEF	CE
M20351	HQTRS CO LAW ENF BN III MHG III MEF	CE
M14052	H&S CO AT BN 4TH MARDIV MARFORRES	CE
M14054	SPT CO (-) AT BN 4TH MARDIV MARFORRES	CE
M14055	SCT PLT SPT CO AT BN 4TH MARDIV MARFORRES	CE
M14056	MG PLT SPT CO AT BN 4TH MARDIV MARFORRES	CE
M14057	AT CO A AT BN 4TH MARDIV MARFORRES	CE
M14061	AT CO C AT BN 4TH MARDIV MARFORRES	CE
M14059	AT CO B (-) AT BN 4TH MARDIV MARFORRES	CE
M14063	AT CO D (-) AT BN 4TH MARDIV MARFORRES	CE
M14066	AT CO E (-) AT BN 4TH MARDIV MARFORRES	CE
M14069	AT CO F (-) AT BN 4TH MARDIV MARFORRES	CE
M14064	2D/3D PLT AT CO D AT BN 4TH MARDIV MARFORRES	CE
M14067	2D/3D PLT AT CO E AT BN 4TH MARDIV MARFORRES	CE
M14070	2D/3D PLT AT CO F AT BN 4TH MARDIV MARFORRES	CE
M14060	3D PLT AT CO B AT BN 4TH MARDIV MARFORRES	CE
M53515	HQTRS CO MCSF REGT	CE
M53541	1ST FAST CO MCSF REGT	CE
M53542	2D FAST CO MCSF REGT	CE
M53543	3D FAST CO MCSF REGT	CE
M53544	FAST CO CENTRAL MCSF REGT	CE
M53545	FAST CO EUROPE MCSF REGT	CE
M53551	MCSF TRNG CO MCSF REGT	CE
M20363	SOTG MHG I MEF	CE
M20136	SOTG MHG II MEF	CE

Enclosure (2)

M20382	SOTG MHG III MEF	CE
M20192	3D CIV AFF GRP MARFORRES	CE
M20193	4TH CIV AFF GRP MARFORRES	CE
M20008	MCSCG MARFORCOM	CE
M87191	SITE SPT (ALAMEDA) HQTRS MARFORRES	CE
M84266	SITE SPT (AMARILLO) HQTRS MARFORRES	CE
M80291	SITE SPT (AMITYVILLE) HQTRS MARFORRES	CE
M87050	SITE SPT (ANCHORAGE) HQTRS MARFORRES	CE
M87278	SITE SPT (BELL) HQTRS MARFORRES	CE
M83220	SITE SPT (BESSEMER) HQTRS MARFORRES	CE
M87248	SITE SPT (BILLINGS) HQTRS MARFORRES	CE
M80292	SITE SPT (BROOKLYN) HQTRS MARFORRES	CE
M20123	SITE SPT (CAMPEN) HQTRS MARFORRES	CE
M80222	SITE SPT (CHICOPEE) HQTRS MARFORRES	CE
M83219	SITE SPT (JACKSON) HQTRS MARFORRES	CE
M87274	SITE SPT (KANEOHE) HQTRS MARFORRES	CE
M84286	SITE SPT (LAFAYETTE) HQTRS MARFORRES	CE
M83273	SITE SPT (MOBILE) HQTRS MARFORRES	CE
M87237	SITE SPT (RENO) HQTRS MARFORRES	CE
M80173	SITE SPT (ROCHESTER) HQTRS MARFORRES	CE
M83314	SITE SPT (TALLAHASSEE) HQTRS MARFORRES	CE
M83251	SITE SPT (W PALM BEACH) HQTRS MARFORRES	CE
M82271	SITE SPT (WASH DC) HQTRS MARFORRES	CE
M30050	MARINE CORPS INFO OPS CENTER (MCIOC)	CE
M11015	DIV HQTRS 1ST MARDIV	GCE
M12002	DIV HQTRS 2D MARDIV	GCE
M13004	DIV HQTRS 3D MARDIV	GCE
M26383	DIV HQTRS 4TH MARDIV	GCE
M11002	HQTRS CO HQTRS BN 1ST MARDIV	GCE
M12012	HQTRS CO HQTRS BN 2D MARDIV	GCE
M13002	HQTRS CO HQTRS BN 3D MARDIV	GCE
M14002	HQTRS CO HQTRS BN 4TH MARDIV	GCE
M11104	HQTRS CO 1ST MAR REGT 1ST MARDIV	GCE
M14101	HQTRS CO 23D MAR REGT 4TH MARDIV	GCE
M14151	HQTRS CO 24TH MAR REGT 4TH MARDIV	GCE
M14201	HQTRS CO 25TH MAR REGT 4TH MARDIV	GCE
M12101	HQTRS CO 2D MAR REGT 2D MARDIV	GCE
M13101	HQTRS CO 3D MAR REGT 3D MARDIV	GCE
M13201	HQTRS CO 4TH MAR REGT 3D MARDIV	GCE
M11154	HQTRS CO 5TH MAR REGT 1ST MARDIV	GCE
M12151	HQTRS CO 6TH MAR REGT 2D MARDIV	GCE
M11204	HQTRS CO 7TH MAR REGT 1ST MARDIV	GCE
M12201	HQTRS CO 8TH MAR REGT 2D MARDIV	GCE
M11111	H&S CO 1/1 1ST MARDIV	GCE
M12111	H&S CO 1/2 2D MARDIV	GCE
M14111	H&S CO 1/23 4TH MARDIV	GCE
M14161	H&S CO 1/24 4TH MARDIV	GCE
M14211	H&S CO 1/25 4TH MARDIV	GCE
M13111	H&S CO 1/3 3D MARDIV	GCE

M11121	H&S CO 1/4 1ST MARDIV	GCE
M11161	H&S CO 1/5 1ST MARDIV	GCE
M12161	H&S CO 1/6 2D MARDIV	GCE
M11211	H&S CO 1/7 1ST MARDIV	GCE
M12211	H&S CO 1/8 2D MARDIV	GCE
M12261	H&S CO 1/9 2D MARDIV	GCE
M13211	H&S CO 2/1 1ST MARDIV	GCE
M12121	H&S CO 2/2 2D MARDIV	GCE
M14121	H&S CO 2/23 4TH MARDIV	GCE
M14171	H&S CO 2/24 4TH MARDIV	GCE
M14221	H&S CO 2/25 4TH MARDIV	GCE
M13124	H&S CO 2/3 3D MARDIV	GCE
M13221	H&S CO 2/4 1ST MARDIV	GCE
M11171	H&S CO 2/5 1ST MARDIV	GCE
M13171	H&S CO 2/6 2D MARDIV	GCE
M11221	H&S CO 2/7 1ST MARDIV	GCE
M12171	H&S CO 2/8 2D MARDIV	GCE
M11141	H&S CO 2/9 2D MARDIV	GCE
M11131	H&S CO 3/1 1ST MARDIV	GCE
M12131	H&S CO 3/2 2D MARDIV	GCE
M14131	H&S CO 3/23 4TH MARDIV	GCE
M14181	H&S CO 3/24 4TH MARDIV	GCE
M14231	H&S CO 3/25 4TH MARDIV	GCE
M13134	H&S CO 3/3 3D MARDIV	GCE
M13231	H&S CO 3/4 1ST MARDIV	GCE
M11181	H&S CO 3/5 1ST MARDIV	GCE
M12181	H&S CO 3/6 2D MARDIV	GCE
M13161	H&S CO 3/7 1ST MARDIV	GCE
M12231	H&S CO 3/8 2D MARDIV	GCE
M12141	H&S CO 3/9 2D MARDIV	GCE
M11113	RFL CO A 1/1 1ST MARDIV	GCE
M12113	RFL CO A 1/2 2D MARDIV	GCE
M14116	RFL CO A 1/23 4TH MARDIV	GCE
M14163	RFL CO A 1/24 4TH MARDIV	GCE
M14212	RFL CO A 1/25 4TH MARDIV	GCE
M13113	RFL CO A 1/3 3D MARDIV	GCE
M11123	RFL CO A 1/4 1ST MARDIV	GCE
M11163	RFL CO A 1/5 1ST MARDIV	GCE
M12163	RFL CO A 1/6 2D MARDIV	GCE
M11213	RFL CO A 1/7 1ST MARDIV	GCE
M12213	RFL CO A 1/8 2D MARDIV	GCE
M12263	RFL CO A 1/9 2D MARDIV	GCE
M11114	RFL CO B 1/1 1ST MARDIV	GCE
M12114	RFL CO B 1/2 2D MARDIV	GCE
M14114	RFL CO B 1/23 4TH MARDIV	GCE
M14168	RFL CO B 1/24 4TH MARDIV	GCE
M14218	RFL CO B 1/25 4TH MARDIV	GCE
M13114	RFL CO B 1/3 3D MARDIV	GCE
M11124	RFL CO B 1/4 1ST MARDIV	GCE

M11164	RFL CO B 1/5 1ST MARDIV	GCE
M12164	RFL CO B 1/6 2D MARDIV	GCE
M11214	RFL CO B 1/7 1ST MARDIV	GCE
M12214	RFL CO B 1/8 2D MARDIV	GCE
M12264	RFL CO B 1/9 2D MARDIV	GCE
M11115	RFL CO C 1/1 1ST MARDIV	GCE
M12115	RFL CO C 1/2 2D MARDIV	GCE
M14115	RFL CO C 1/23 4TH MARDIV	GCE
M14165	RFL CO C 1/24 4TH MARDIV	GCE
M14214	RFL CO C 1/25 4TH MARDIV	GCE
M13115	RFL CO C 1/3 3D MARDIV	GCE
M11125	RFL CO C 1/4 1ST MARDIV	GCE
M11165	RFL CO C 1/5 1ST MARDIV	GCE
M12165	RFL CO C 1/6 2D MARDIV	GCE
M11215	RFL CO C 1/7 1ST MARDIV	GCE
M12215	RFL CO C 1/8 2D MARDIV	GCE
M12265	RFL CO C 1/9 2D MARDIV	GCE
M13213	RFL CO E 2/1 1ST MARDIV	GCE
M12124	RFL CO E 2/2 2D MARDIV	GCE
M14126	RFL CO E 2/23 4TH MARDIV	GCE
M14173	RFL CO E 2/24 4TH MARDIV	GCE
M14226	RFL CO E 2/25 4TH MARDIV	GCE
M13121	RFL CO E 2/3 3D MARDIV	GCE
M13224	RFL CO E 2/4 1ST MARDIV	GCE
M11174	RFL CO E 2/5 1ST MARDIV	GCE
M13174	RFL CO E 2/6 2D MARDIV	GCE
M11224	RFL CO E 2/7 1ST MARDIV	GCE
M12174	RFL CO E 2/8 2D MARDIV	GCE
M11143	RFL CO E 2/9 2D MARDIV	GCE
M13214	RFL CO F 2/1 1ST MARDIV	GCE
M12125	RFL CO F 2/2 2D MARDIV	GCE
M14124	RFL CO F 2/23 4TH MARDIV	GCE
M14174	RFL CO F 2/24 4TH MARDIV	GCE
M14224	RFL CO F 2/25 4TH MARDIV	GCE
M13122	RFL CO F 2/3 3D MARDIV	GCE
M13225	RFL CO F 2/4 1ST MARDIV	GCE
M11175	RFL CO F 2/5 1ST MARDIV	GCE
M13175	RFL CO F 2/6 2D MARDIV	GCE
M11225	RFL CO F 2/7 1ST MARDIV	GCE
M12175	RFL CO F 2/8 2D MARDIV	GCE
M11144	RFL CO F 2/9 2D MARDIV	GCE
M13215	RFL CO G 2/1 1ST MARDIV	GCE
M12126	RFL CO G 2/2 2D MARDIV	GCE
M14125	RFL CO G 2/23 4TH MARDIV	GCE
M14175	RFL CO G 2/24 4TH MARDIV	GCE
M14225	RFL CO G 2/25 4TH MARDIV	GCE
M13123	RFL CO G 2/3 3D MARDIV	GCE
M13226	RFL CO G 2/4 1ST MARDIV	GCE
M11176	RFL CO G 2/5 1ST MARDIV	GCE

Enclosure (2)

M13176	RFL CO G 2/6 2D MARDIV	GCE
M11226	RFL CO G 2/7 1ST MARDIV	GCE
M12176	RFL CO G 2/8 2D MARDIV	GCE
M11145	RFL CO G 2/9 2D MARDIV	GCE
M11135	RFL CO I 3/1 1ST MARDIV	GCE
M12135	RFL CO I 3/2 2D MARDIV	GCE
M14136	RFL CO I 3/23 4TH MARDIV	GCE
M14183	RFL CO I 3/24 4TH MARDIV	GCE
M14216	RFL CO I 3/25 4TH MARDIV	GCE
M13131	RFL CO I 3/3 3D MARDIV	GCE
M13234	RFL CO I 3/4 1ST MARDIV	GCE
M11185	RFL CO I 3/5 1ST MARDIV	GCE
M12185	RFL CO I 3/6 2D MARDIV	GCE
M13163	RFL CO I 3/7 1ST MARDIV	GCE
M12235	RFL CO I 3/8 2D MARDIV	GCE
M12143	RFL CO I 3/9 2D MARDIV	GCE
M11136	RFL CO K 3/1 1ST MARDIV	GCE
M12136	RFL CO K 3/2 2D MARDIV	GCE
M14134	RFL CO K 3/23 4TH MARDIV	GCE
M14184	RFL CO K 3/24 4TH MARDIV	GCE
M14234	RFL CO K 3/25 4TH MARDIV	GCE
M13132	RFL CO K 3/3 3D MARDIV	GCE
M13236	RFL CO K 3/4 1ST MARDIV	GCE
M11186	RFL CO K 3/5 1ST MARDIV	GCE
M12186	RFL CO K 3/6 2D MARDIV	GCE
M13164	RFL CO K 3/7 1ST MARDIV	GCE
M12236	RFL CO K 3/8 2D MARDIV	GCE
M12144	RFL CO K 3/9 2D MARDIV	GCE
M11137	RFL CO L 3/1 1ST MARDIV	GCE
M12137	RFL CO L 3/2 2D MARDIV	GCE
M14138	RFL CO L 3/23 4TH MARDIV	GCE
M14182	RFL CO L 3/24 4TH MARDIV	GCE
M14236	RFL CO L 3/25 4TH MARDIV	GCE
M13133	RFL CO L 3/3 3D MARDIV	GCE
M13237	RFL CO L 3/4 1ST MARDIV	GCE
M11187	RFL CO L 3/5 1ST MARDIV	GCE
M12187	RFL CO L 3/6 2D MARDIV	GCE
M13165	RFL CO L 3/7 1ST MARDIV	GCE
M12238	RFL CO L 3/8 2D MARDIV	GCE
M12145	RFL CO L 3/9 2D MARDIV	GCE
M11112	WPNS CO 1/1 1ST MARDIV	GCE
M12112	WPNS CO 1/2 2D MARDIV	GCE
M14133	WPNS CO 1/23 4TH MARDIV	GCE
M14167	WPNS CO 1/24 4TH MARDIV	GCE
M14217	WPNS CO 1/25 4TH MARDIV	GCE
M13112	WPNS CO 1/3 3D MARDIV	GCE
M11122	WPNS CO 1/4 1ST MARDIV	GCE
M11162	WPNS CO 1/5 1ST MARDIV	GCE
M12162	WPNS CO 1/6 2D MARDIV	GCE

Enclosure (2)

M11212	WPNS CO 1/7 1ST MARDIV	GCE
M12212	WPNS CO 1/8 2D MARDIV	GCE
M12262	WPNS CO 1/9 2D MARDIV	GCE
M13212	WPNS CO 2/1 1ST MARDIV	GCE
M12122	WPNS CO 2/2 2D MARDIV	GCE
M14127	WPNS CO 2/23 4TH MARDIV	GCE
M14176	WPNS CO 2/24 4TH MARDIV	GCE
M14227	WPNS CO 2/25 4TH MARDIV	GCE
M13125	WPNS CO 2/3 3D MARDIV	GCE
M13222	WPNS CO 2/4 1ST MARDIV	GCE
M11172	WPNS CO 2/5 1ST MARDIV	GCE
M13173	WPNS CO 2/6 2D MARDIV	GCE
M11222	WPNS CO 2/7 1ST MARDIV	GCE
M12172	WPNS CO 2/8 2D MARDIV	GCE
M11142	WPNS CO 2/9 2D MARDIV	GCE
M11132	WPNS CO 3/1 1ST MARDIV	GCE
M12132	WPNS CO 3/2 2D MARDIV	GCE
M14137	WPNS CO 3/23 4TH MARDIV	GCE
M14186	WPNS CO 3/24 4TH MARDIV	GCE
M14237	WPNS CO 3/25 4TH MARDIV	GCE
M13135	WPNS CO 3/3 3D MARDIV	GCE
M13232	WPNS CO 3/4 1ST MARDIV	GCE
M11182	WPNS CO 3/5 1ST MARDIV	GCE
M12182	WPNS CO 3/6 2D MARDIV	GCE
M13162	WPNS CO 3/7 1ST MARDIV	GCE
M12232	WPNS CO 3/8 2D MARDIV	GCE
M12142	WPNS CO 3/9 2D MARDIV	GCE
M14621	HQTRS BTRY 2/14 4TH MARDIV	GCE
M11351	HQTRS BTRY 5/11 1ST MARDIV	GCE
M14622	RCKT BTRY D 2/14 4TH MARDIV	GCE
M14623	RCKT BTRY F 2/14 4TH MARDIV	GCE
M14624	RCKT BTRY K 2/14 4TH MARDIV	GCE
M11355	RCKT BTRY Q 5/11 1ST MARDIV	GCE
M11352	RCKT BTRY R 5/11 1ST MARDIV	GCE
M11353	RCKT BTRY S 5/11 1ST MARDIV	GCE
M11354	RCKT BTRY T 5/11 1ST MARDIV	GCE
M12313	ARTY BTRY A 1/10 2D MARDIV	GCE
M11313	ARTY BTRY A 1/11 1ST MARDIV	GCE
M13312	ARTY BTRY A 1/12 3D MARDIV	GCE
M12314	ARTY BTRY B 1/10 2D MARDIV	GCE
M11314	ARTY BTRY B 1/11 1ST MARDIV	GCE
M13313	ARTY BTRY B 1/12 3D MARDIV	GCE
M12315	ARTY BTRY C 1/10 2D MARDIV	GCE
M11315	ARTY BTRY C 1/11 1ST MARDIV	GCE
M13314	ARTY BTRY C 1/12 3D MARDIV	GCE
M12323	ARTY BTRY E 2/10 2D MARDIV	GCE
M11323	ARTY BTRY E 2/11 1ST MARDIV	GCE
M12362	ARTY BTRY E 2/12 3D MARDIV	GCE
M12324	ARTY BTRY F 2/10 2D MARDIV	GCE

M11324	ARTY BTRY F 2/11 1ST MARDIV	GCE
M12363	ARTY BTRY F 2/12 2D MARDIV	GCE
M12325	ARTY BTRY G 2/10 2D MARDIV	GCE
M11325	ARTY BTRY G 2/11 1ST MARDIV	GCE
M14333	ARTY BTRY G 3/14 4TH MARDIV	GCE
M14334	ARTY BTRY H 3/14 4TH MARDIV	GCE
M12333	ARTY BTRY I 3/10 2D MARDIV	GCE
M11333	ARTY BTRY I 3/11 1ST MARDIV	GCE
M12356	ARTY BTRY I 3/12 1ST MARDIV	GCE
M14335	ARTY BTRY I 3/14 4TH MARDIV	GCE
M12334	ARTY BTRY K 3/10 2D MARDIV	GCE
M11334	ARTY BTRY K 3/11 1ST MARDIV	GCE
M11326	ARTY BTRY K 3/12 1ST MARDIV	GCE
M12335	ARTY BTRY L 3/10 2D MARDIV	GCE
M13336	ARTY BTRY L 3/12 1ST MARDIV	GCE
M11335	ARTY BTRY M 3/11 1ST MARDIV	GCE
M14345	ARTY BTRY M 3/14 4TH MARDIV	GCE
M14352	ARTY BTRY N 5/14 4TH MARDIV	GCE
M14643	ARTY BTRY O 5/14 4TH MARDIV	GCE
M14354	ARTY BTRY P 5/14 4TH MARDIV	GCE
M14313	ARTY BTRY Q 5/14 4TH MARDIV	GCE
M12311	HQTRS BTRY 1/10 2D MARDIV	GCE
M11316	HQTRS BTRY 1/11 1ST MARDIV	GCE
M13311	HQTRS BTRY 1/12 3D MARDIV	GCE
M12321	HQTRS BTRY 2/10 2D MARDIV	GCE
M11321	HQTRS BTRY 2/11 1ST MARDIV	GCE
M12331	HQTRS BTRY 3/10 2D MARDIV	GCE
M11331	HQTRS BTRY 3/11 1ST MARDIV	GCE
M13331	HQTRS BTRY 3/12 3D MARDIV	GCE
M14331	HQTRS BTRY 3/14 4TH MARDIV	GCE
M14641	HQTRS BTRY 5/14 4TH MARDIV	GCE
M13301	HQTRS BTRY (-) 12TH MAR REGT 3D MARDIV	GCE
M12301	HQTRS BTRY 10TH MAR REGT 2D MARDIV	GCE
M11303	HQTRS BTRY 11TH MAR REGT 1ST MARDIV	GCE
M14301	HQTRS BTRY 14TH MAR REGT 4TH MARDIV	GCE
M13320	DET HQTRS BTRY 12TH MAR 3D MARDIV	GCE
M21411	H&S CO 1ST TANK BN 1ST MARDIV	GCE
M21421	H&S CO 2D TANK BN 2D MARDIV	GCE
M21441	H&S CO 4TH TANK BN 4TH MARDIV	GCE
M21412	TANK CO A 1ST TANK BN 1ST MARDIV	GCE
M21422	TANK CO A 2D TANK BN 2D MARDIV	GCE
M21442	TANK CO A 4TH TANK BN 4TH MARDIV	GCE
M21413	TANK CO B 1ST TANK BN 1ST MARDIV	GCE
M21423	TANK CO B 2D TANK BN 2D MARDIV	GCE
M21443	TANK CO B 4TH TANK BN 4TH MARDIV	GCE
M21414	TANK CO C 1ST TANK BN 1ST MARDIV	GCE
M21424	TANK CO C 2D TANK BN 2D MARDIV	GCE
M21444	TANK CO C 4TH TANK BN 4TH MARDIV	GCE
M21415	TANK CO D 1ST TANK BN 1ST MARDIV	GCE

Enclosure (2)

M21425	TANK CO D 2D TANK BN 2D MARDIV	GCE
M21445	TANK CO D 4TH TANK BN 4TH MARDIV	GCE
M21403	TANK CO E 4TH TANK BN 4TH MARDIV	GCE
M21405	TANK CO F 4TH TANK BN 4TH MARDIV	GCE
M21811	H&S CO 2D AAV BN 2D MARDIV	GCE
M21821	H&S CO 3D AAV BN 1ST MARDIV	GCE
M21831	H&S CO 4TH AAV BN 4TH MARDIV	GCE
M21812	AAV CO A 2D AAV BN 2D MARDIV	GCE
M21822	AAV CO A 3D AAV BN 1ST MARDIV	GCE
M21834	AAV CO A 4TH AAV BN 4TH MARDIV	GCE
M21813	AAV CO B 2D AAV BN 2D MARDIV	GCE
M21823	AAV CO B 3D AAV BN 1ST MARDIV	GCE
M21883	AAV CO B 4TH AAV BN 4TH MARDIV	GCE
M21814	AAV CO C 2D AAV BN 2D MARDIV	GCE
M21824	AAV CO C 3D AAV BN 1ST MARDIV	GCE
M21815	AAV CO D 2D AAV BN 2D MARDIV	GCE
M21825	AAV CO D 3D AAV BN 1ST MARDIV	GCE
M21827	AAV CO E (REIN) 3D AAV BN 1ST MARDIV	GCE
M11401	H&S CO 1ST CEB 1ST MARDIV	GCE
M12401	H&S CO 2D CEB 2D MARDIV	GCE
M13421	H&S CO 3D CEB 3D MARDIV	GCE
M14401	H&S CO 4TH CEB 4TH MARDIV	GCE
M11407	ENGR SPT CO 1ST CEB 1ST MARDIV	GCE
M12407	ENGR SPT CO 2D CEB 2D MARDIV	GCE
M13422	ENGR SPT CO 3D CEB 3D MARDIV	GCE
M14407	ENGR SPT CO 4TH CEB 4TH MARDIV	GCE
M11403	COMBAT ENGR CO A 1ST CEB 1ST MARDIV	GCE
M12403	COMBAT ENGR CO A 2D CEB 2D MARDIV	GCE
M13423	COMBAT ENGR CO A 3D CEB 3D MARDIV	GCE
M14403	COMBAT ENGR CO A 4TH CEB 4TH MARDIV	GCE
M11404	COMBAT ENGR CO B 1ST CEB 1ST MARDIV	GCE
M12404	COMBAT ENGR CO B 2D CEB 2D MARDIV	GCE
M13424	COMBAT ENGR CO B 3D CEB 3D MARDIV	GCE
M14404	COMBAT ENGR CO B 4TH CEB 4TH MARDIV	GCE
M11405	COMBAT ENGR CO C 1ST CEB 1ST MARDIV	GCE
M12405	COMBAT ENGR CO C 2D CEB 2D MARDIV	GCE
M14405	COMBAT ENGR CO C 4TH CEB 4TH MARDIV	GCE
M14406	COMBAT ENGR CO D 4TH CEB 4TH MARDIV	GCE
M11406	COMBAT ENGR CO D (W/ABV PLT) 1ST CEB 1ST MARDIV	GCE
M12406	COMBAT ENGR CO D (W/ABV PLT) 2D CEB 2D MARDIV	GCE
M21804	ENGR CO 3D CAB 3D MARDIV	GCE
M21801	H&S CO 3D CAB 3D MARDIV	GCE
M11006	COMM CO HQTRS BN 1ST MARDIV	GCE
M12003	COMM CO HQTRS BN 2D MARDIV	GCE
M13006	COMM CO HQTRS BN 3D MARDIV	GCE
M14004	COMM CO HQTRS BN 4TH MARDIV	GCE
M13009	1ST SP SEC COMM TM HQTRS BN 3D MARDIV	GCE
M11016	2D SP SEC COMM TM HQTRS BN 1ST MARDIV	GCE
M12004	5TH SP SEC COMM TM HQTRS BN 2D MARDIV	GCE

Enclosure (2)

M11017	DS TM 1 HQTRS BN 1ST MARDIV	GCE
M12007	DS TM 1 HQTRS BN 2D MARDIV	GCE
M13005	DS TM 1 HQTRS BN 3D MARDIV	GCE
M11018	DS TM 2 HQTRS BN 1ST MARDIV	GCE
M12006	DS TM 2 HQTRS BN 2D MARDIV	GCE
M13008	DS TM 2 HQTRS BN 3D MARDIV	GCE
M11019	DS TM 3 HQTRS BN 1ST MARDIV	GCE
M12011	DS TM 3 HQTRS BN 2D MARDIV	GCE
M14102	DS TM 23D MAR REGT 4TH MARDIV	GCE
M14152	DS TM 24TH MAR REGT 4TH MARDIV	GCE
M14202	DS TM 25TH MAR REGT 4TH MARDIV	GCE
M11702	LAR CO A 1ST LAR BN 1ST MARDIV	GCE
M12192	LAR CO A 2D LAR BN 2D MARDIV	GCE
M13702	LAR CO A 3D LAR BN 1ST MARDIV	GCE
M14032	LAR CO A 4TH LAR BN 4TH MARDIV	GCE
M11703	LAR CO B 1ST LAR BN 1ST MARDIV	GCE
M12193	LAR CO B 2D LAR BN 2D MARDIV	GCE
M13703	LAR CO B 3D LAR BN 1ST MARDIV	GCE
M14033	LAR CO B 4TH LAR BN 4TH MARDIV	GCE
M11704	LAR CO C 1ST LAR BN 1ST MARDIV	GCE
M12194	LAR CO C 2D LAR BN 2D MARDIV	GCE
M13704	LAR CO C 3D LAR BN 1ST MARDIV	GCE
M14034	LAR CO C 4TH LAR BN 4TH MARDIV	GCE
M11705	LAR CO D 1ST LAR BN 1ST MARDIV	GCE
M12195	LAR CO D 2D LAR BN 2D MARDIV	GCE
M13708	LAR CO D 3D LAR BN 1ST MARDIV	GCE
M14035	LAR CO D 4TH LAR BN 4TH MARDIV	GCE
M11706	LAR CO E 1ST LAR BN 1ST MARDIV	GCE
M12196	LAR CO E 2D LAR BN 2D MARDIV	GCE
M13709	LAR CO E 3D LAR BN 1ST MARDIV	GCE
M14040	LAR CO E 4TH LAR BN 4TH MARDIV	GCE
M14041	LAR CO F 4TH LAR BN 4TH MARDIV	GCE
M11701	H&S CO 1ST LAR BN 1ST MARDIV	GCE
M12191	H&S CO 2D LAR BN 2D MARDIV	GCE
M13701	H&S CO 3D LAR BN 1ST MARDIV	GCE
M14031	H&S CO 4TH LAR BN 4TH MARDIV	GCE
M13007	JWTC HQTRS BN 3D MARDIV	GCE
M13403	CMBT ASLT CO 3D MAR REGT 3D MARDIV	GCE
M11014	1ST MARDIV BAND 1ST MARDIV	GCE
M12005	2D MARDIV BAND 2D MARDIV	GCE
M11011	RECON CO A 1ST RECON BN 1ST MARDIV	GCE
M12017	RECON CO A 2D RECON BN 2D MARDIV	GCE
M14702	RECON CO A 4TH RECON BN 4TH MARDIV	GCE
M11012	RECON CO B 1ST RECON BN 1ST MARDIV	GCE
M12018	RECON CO B 2D RECON BN 2D MARDIV	GCE
M14703	RECON CO B 4TH RECON BN 4TH MARDIV	GCE
M11013	RECON CO C 1ST RECON BN 1ST MARDIV	GCE
M12019	RECON CO C 2D RECON BN 2D MARDIV	GCE
M14706	RECON CO C 4TH RECON BN 4TH MARDIV	GCE

Enclosure (2)

M14705	RECON CO D 4TH RECON BN 4TH MARDIV	GCE
M14707	RECON CO E 4TH RECON BN 4TH MARDIV	GCE
M11007	FORCE RECON CO 1ST RECON BN 1ST MARDIV I MEF	GCE
M12014	FORCE RECON CO 2D RECON BN 2D MARDIV II MEF	GCE
M13014	FORCE RECON CO 3D RECON BN 3D MARDIV III MEF	GCE
M11010	H&S CO 1ST RECON BN 1ST MARDIV	GCE
M12016	H&S CO 2D RECON BN 2D MARDIV	GCE
M13012	H&S CO 3D RECON BN 3D MARDIV	GCE
M14701	H&S CO 4TH RECON BN 4TH MARDIV	GCE
M13013	DISTANT RECON CO 3D RECON BN 3D MARDIV	GCE
M14003	MP CO HQTRS BN 4TH MARDIV	GCE
M11008	TRUCK CO A HQTRS BN 1ST MARDIV	GCE
M12008	TRUCK CO A HQTRS BN 2D MARDIV	GCE
M11030	TRUCK CO B HQTRS BN 1ST MARDIV	GCE
M12030	TRUCK CO B HQTRS BN 2D MARDIV	GCE
M13010	TRUCK CO HQTRS BN 3D MARDIV	GCE
M14662	TRUCK CO HQTRS BN 4TH MARDIV	GCE
M87224	SITE SPT (29 PALMS) 4TH TANK BN 4TH MARDIV	GCE
M81240	SITE SPT (ALLENTOWN)	GCE
M83410	SITE SPT (ATLANTA) 4TH RECON BN 4TH MARDIV	GCE
M85252	SITE SPT (AURORA) 14TH MAR REGT 4TH MARDIV	GCE
M84221	SITE SPT (AUSTIN) 23D MAR REGT 4TH MARDIV	GCE
M82220	SITE SPT (BALTIMORE) 4TH CEB 4TH MARDIV	GCE
M84282	SITE SPT (BATON ROUGE)	GCE
M87296	SITE SPT (BOISE) 4TH TANK BN 4TH MARDIV	GCE
M84283	SITE SPT (BOSSIER CITY) 23D MAR REGT 4TH MARDIV	GCE
M85295	SITE SPT (BRIDGETON) 24TH MAR REGT 4TH MARDIV	GCE
M81230	SITE SPT (BRISTOL) 14TH MAR REGT 4TH MARDIV	GCE
M84259	SITE SPT (BROKEN ARROW)	GCE
M81225	SITE SPT (BROOK PARK) 25TH MAR REGT 4TH MARDIV	GCE
M80251	SITE SPT (BRUNSWICK)	GCE
M80242	SITE SPT (BUFFALO) 25TH MAR REGT 4TH MARDIV	GCE
M82231	SITE SPT (CAMLEJ) 4TH TANK BN 4TH MARDIV	GCE
M87283	SITE SPT (CAMPEN) 4TH LAR BN 4TH MARDIV	GCE
M82223	SITE SPT (CHARLESTON) 4TH CEB 4TH MARDIV	GCE
M83222	SITE SPT (CHATTANOOGA) 14TH MAR REGT 4TH MARDIV	GCE
M85225	SITE SPT (CHICAGO) 24TH MAR REGT 4TH MARDIV	GCE
M81220	SITE SPT (CINCINNATI) HQTRS BN 4TH MARDIV	GCE
M83301	SITE SPT (COLUMBIA) 4TH LAR BN 4TH MARDIV	GCE
M81227	SITE SPT (COLUMBUS) 25TH MAR REGT 4TH MARDIV	GCE
M84222	SITE SPT (CORPUS CHRISTI) 23D MAR REGT 4TH MARDIV	GCE
M85233	SITE SPT (DES MOINES) 24TH MAR REGT 4TH MARDIV	GCE
M80227	SITE SPT (DOVER) 25TH MAR REGT 4TH MARDIV	GCE
M81252	SITE SPT (EBENSBURG) HQTRS BN 4TH MARDIV	GCE
M84260	SITE SPT (EL PASO) 14TH MAR REGT 4TH MARDIV	GCE
M84220	SITE SPT (ELLINGTON) 23D MAR REGT 4TH MARDIV	GCE
M81180	SITE SPT (ERIE) HQTRS BN 4TH MARDIV	GCE
M85227	SITE SPT (FORT SHERIDAN) 24TH MAR REGT 4TH MARDIV	GCE
M82090	SITE SPT (FT DETRICK) 4TH LAR BN 4TH MARDIV	GCE

M80220	SITE SPT (FT DEVENS) 25TH MAR REGT 4TH MARDIV	GCE
M81233	SITE SPT (FT DIX) 14TH MAR REGT 4TH MARDIV	GCE
M82230	SITE SPT (FT KNOX) 4TH TANK BN 4TH MARDIV	GCE
M84236	SITE SPT (FT WORTH) 14TH MAR REGT 4TH MARDIV	GCE
M84267	SITE SPT (GALVESTON) 4TH AAV BN 4TH MARDIV	GCE
M80225	SITE SPT (GARDEN CITY) 25TH MAR REGT 4TH MARDIV	GCE
M80228	SITE SPT (GLENVILLE) 25TH MAR REGT 4TH MARDIV	GCE
M84142	SITE SPT (GRAND PRAIRIE) 14TH MAR REGT 4TH MARDIV	GCE
M85224	SITE SPT (GRAND RAPIDS) 24TH MAR REGT 4TH MARDIV	GCE
M83279	SITE SPT (GULFPORT) 4TH AAV BN 4TH MARDIV	GCE
M84140	SITE SPT (HARLINGEN) 23D MAR REGT 4TH MARDIV	GCE
M81269	SITE SPT (HARRISBURG) 25TH MAR REGT 4TH MARDIV	GCE
M83185	SITE SPT (HUNTSVILLE) 4TH MARDIV	GCE
M85218	SITE SPT (INDIANAPOLIS) HQTRS BN 4TH MARDIV	GCE
M83276	SITE SPT (JACKSONVILLE) 4TH AAV BN 4TH MARDIV	GCE
M83269	SITE SPT (JOHNSON CITY) 24TH MAR REGT 4TH MARDIV	GCE
M85232	SITE SPT (JOLIET) 4TH RECON BN 4TH MARDIV	GCE
M85217	SITE SPT (KANSAS CITY) 24TH MAR REGT 4TH MARDIV	GCE
M84243	SITE SPT (KIRTLAND AFB) 4TH RECON BN 4TH MARDIV	GCE
M83177	SITE SPT (KNOXVILLE) 4TH CEB 4TH MARDIV	GCE
M85222	SITE SPT (LANSING) 24TH MAR REGT 4TH MARDIV	GCE
M87249	SITE SPT (LAS VEGAS) 23D MAR REGT 4TH MARDIV	GCE
M82229	SITE SPT (LITTLE CREEK) 4TH AAV BN 4TH MARDIV	GCE
M84284	SITE SPT (LITTLE ROCK) 23D MAR REGT 4TH MARDIV	GCE
M87222	SITE SPT (LOS ALAMITOS) 23D MAR REGT 4TH MARDIV	GCE
M82221	SITE SPT (LYNCHBURG) 4TH CEB 4TH MARDIV	GCE
M85229	SITE SPT (MADISON)	GCE
M80223	SITE SPT (MANCHESTER) 25TH MAR REGT 4TH MARDIV	GCE
M83263	SITE SPT (MEMPHIS) 23D MAR REGT 4TH MARDIV	GCE
M83285	SITE SPT (MIAMI) 4TH TANK BN 4TH MARDIV	GCE
M85228	SITE SPT (MILWAUKEE) 24TH MAR REGT 4TH MARDIV	GCE
M85230	SITE SPT (MINNEAPOLIS) HQTRS BN 4TH MARDIV	GCE
M83303	SITE SPT (MONTGOMERY) 23D MAR REGT 4TH MARDIV	GCE
M82270	SITE SPT (N VERSAILLES) 25TH MAR REGT 4TH MARDIV	GCE
M84281	SITE SPT (NEW ORLEANS) 23D MAR REGT 4TH MARDIV	GCE
M81226	SITE SPT (NORTH CANTON)	GCE
M87256	SITE SPT (OKLAHOMA) 14TH MAR REGT 4TH MARDIV	GCE
M87220	SITE SPT (PASADENA) 23D MAR REGT 4TH MARDIV	GCE
M85221	SITE SPT (PERRYSBURG) 24TH MAR REGT 4TH MARDIV	GCE
M87232	SITE SPT (PICO RIVERA) 14TH MAR REGT 4TH MARDIV	GCE
M80221	SITE SPT (PLAINVILLE) 25TH MAR REGT 4TH MARDIV	GCE
M87223	SITE SPT (PORT HUENEME) 23D MAR REGT 4TH MARDIV	GCE
M82180	SITE SPT (QUANTICO) 4TH LAR BN 4TH MARDIV	GCE
M81234	SITE SPT (RICHMOND) 14TH MAR REGT 4TH MARDIV	GCE
M85240	SITE SPT (RIVERTON) 4TH LAR BN 4TH MARDIV	GCE
M82222	SITE SPT (ROANOKE) 4TH CEB 4TH MARDIV	GCE
M85223	SITE SPT (SAGINAW) 24TH MAR REGT 4TH MARDIV	GCE
M87238	SITE SPT (SALT LAKE CITY) 23D MAR REGT 4TH MARDIV	GCE
M84240	SITE SPT (SAN ANTONIO) 4TH RECON BN 4TH MARDIV	GCE

M87195	SITE SPT (SAN BRUNO) 23D MAR REGT 4TH MARDIV	GCE
M87225	SITE SPT (SAN BRUNO) 23D MAR REGT 4TH MARDIV	GCE
M87272	SITE SPT (SAN DIEGO) 4TH TANK BN 4TH MARDIV	GCE
M87230	SITE SPT (SEAL BEACH) 14TH MAR REGT 4TH MARDIV	GCE
M85220	SITE SPT (SELFRIDGE) 24TH MAR REGT 4TH MARDIV	GCE
M83223	SITE SPT (SMYRNA) 24TH MAR REGT 4TH MARDIV	GCE
M87246	SITE SPT (SPOKANE) 14TH MAR REGT 4TH MARDIV	GCE
M85298	SITE SPT (SPRINGFIELD) 24TH MAR REGT 4TH MARDIV	GCE
M80174	SITE SPT (SYRACUSE) 4TH LAR BN 4TH MARDIV	GCE
M83275	SITE SPT (TAMPA FL) 4TH AAV BN 4TH MARDIV	GCE
M82225	SITE SPT (TERRE HAUTE) 24TH MAR REGT 4TH MARDIV	GCE
M82140	SITE SPT (WAHPETON) HQTRS BN 4TH MARDIV	GCE
M80217	SITE SPT (WORCHESTER) 25TH MAR REGT 4TH MARDIV	GCE
M87297	SITE SPT (YAKIMA) 4TH TANK BN 4TH MARDIV	GCE
M71706	1ST/2D PLT TRUCK CO HQTRS BN 4TH MARDIV	GCE
M14410	DET 1 ENGR SPT CO 4TH CEB 4TH MARDIV	GCE
M21837	DET 1 H&S CO 4TH AAV BN 4TH MARDIV	GCE
M14409	DET 1 H&S CO 4TH CEB 4TH MARDIV	GCE
M14036	DET 1 H&S CO 4TH LAR BN 4TH MARDIV	GCE
M21449	DET 1 H&S CO 4TH TANK BN 4TH MARDIV	GCE
M14412	DET 2 ENGR SPT CO 4TH CEB 4TH MARDIV	GCE
M21838	DET 2 H&S CO 4TH AAV BN 4TH MARDIV	GCE
M14411	DET 2 H&S CO 4TH CEB 4TH MARDIV	GCE
M14037	DET 2 H&S CO 4TH LAR BN 4TH MARDIV	GCE
M14710	DET 2 H&S CO 4TH RECON BN 4TH MARDIV	GCE
M21448	DET 2 H&S CO 4TH TANK BN 4TH MARDIV	GCE
M14414	DET 3 ENGR SPT CO 4TH CEB 4TH MARDIV	GCE
M21833	DET 3 H&S CO 4TH AAV BN 4TH MARDIV	GCE
M14413	DET 3 H&S CO 4TH CEB 4TH MARDIV	GCE
M14038	DET 3 H&S CO 4TH LAR BN 4TH MARDIV	GCE
M21447	DET 3 H&S CO 4TH TANK BN 4TH MARDIV	GCE
M14408	DET 4 ENGR SPT CO 4TH CEB 4TH MARDIV	GCE
M21839	DET 4 H&S CO 4TH AAV BN 4TH MARDIV	GCE
M14415	DET 4 H&S CO 4TH CEB 4TH MARDIV	GCE
M14042	DET 4 H&S CO 4TH LAR BN 4TH MARDIV	GCE
M14712	DET 4 H&S CO 4TH RECON BN 4TH MARDIV	GCE
M21627	DET 4 H&S CO 4TH TANK BN 4TH MARDIV	GCE
M14043	DET 5 H&S CO 4TH LAR BN 4TH MARDIV	GCE
M14713	DET 5 H&S CO 4TH RECON BN 4TH MARDIV	GCE
M21406	DET 5 H&S CO 4TH TANK BN 4TH MARDIV	GCE
M21408	DET 6 H&S CO 4TH TANK BN 4TH MARDIV	GCE
M21832	DET AAV CO A 4TH AAV BN 4TH MARDIV	GCE
M21835	DET AAV CO B 4TH AAV BN 4TH MARDIV	GCE
M75240	DET COMM CO HQTRS BN 4TH MARDIV	GCE
M14018	DET MP CO HQTRS BN 4TH MARDIV	GCE
M22321	H&S CO 6TH ESB 4TH MLG	LCE
M21301	H&S CO 7TH ESB 1ST MLG	LCE
M21311	H&S CO 8TH ESB 2D MLG	LCE
M29101	H&S CO 9TH ESB 3D MLG	LCE

M22324	ENGR SPT CO 6TH ESB 4TH MLG	LCE
M21302	ENGR SPT CO 7TH ESB 1ST MLG	LCE
M21312	ENGR SPT CO 8TH ESB 2D MLG	LCE
M29102	ENGR SPT CO 9TH ESB 3D MLG	LCE
M21306	BRIDGE CO 7TH ESB 1ST MLG	LCE
M21330	BRIDGE CO 8TH ESB 2D MLG	LCE
M21337	BRIDGE CO A 6TH ESB 4TH MLG	LCE
M22317	BRIDGE CO B 6TH ESB 4TH MLG	LCE
M28314	BULK FUEL CO 7TH ESB 1ST MLG	LCE
M27114	BULK FUEL CO 8TH ESB 2D MLG	LCE
M29103	BULK FUEL CO 9TH ESB 3D MLG	LCE
M22429	BULK FUEL CO C 6TH ESB 4TH MLG	LCE
M29063	BULK FUEL CO A (-) 6TH ESB 4TH MLG	LCE
M22428	BULK FUEL CO B (-) 6TH ESB 4TH MLG	LCE
M29319	DET 1 BULK FUEL CO A 6TH ESB 4TH MLG	LCE
M29320	DET 2 BULK FUEL CO A 6TH ESB 4TH MLG	LCE
M29326	DET BULK FUEL CO B 6TH ESB 4TH MLG	LCE
M28117	B FUEL TRANS PLT GS MT CO 6TH MT BN 4TH MLG	LCE
M21303	ENGR CO 7TH ESB 1ST MLG	LCE
M21313	ENGR CO 8TH ESB 2D MLG	LCE
M29104	ENGR CO 9TH ESB 3D MLG	LCE
M77775	ENGR CO A 6TH ESB 4TH MLG	LCE
M22325	ENGR CO B 6TH ESB 4TH MLG	LCE
M21304	ENGR CO B 7TH ESB 1ST MLG	LCE
M21314	ENGR CO B 8TH ESB 2D MLG	LCE
M75301	ENGR CO C 6TH ESB 4TH MLG	LCE
M21305	ENGR CO C 7TH ESB 1ST MLG	LCE
M21315	ENGR CO C 8TH ESB 2D MLG	LCE
M28364	ENGR SVCS CO CLB 1 CLR 1 1ST MLG	LCE
M27344	ENGR SVCS CO CLB 2 CLR 2 2D MLG	LCE
M29039	ENGR SVCS CO CLB 3 CLR 3 3D MLG	LCE
M29047	ENGR SVCS CO CLB 4 CLR 3 3D MLG	LCE
M28266	ENGR SVCS CO CLB 5 CLR 1 1ST MLG	LCE
M27354	ENGR SVCS CO CLB 6 CLR 2 2D MLG	LCE
M28348	ENGR SVCS CO CLB 7 CLR 1 1ST MLG	LCE
M21681	HQTRS CO 6TH COMM BN 4TH MLG	LCE
M21683	DS COMM CO 6TH COMM BN 4TH MLG	LCE
M21685	GS COMM CO 6TH COMM BN 4TH MLG	LCE
M21684	SVC CO 6TH COMM BN 4TH MLG	LCE
M28303	COMM CO CLR 17 1ST MLG	LCE
M27103	COMM CO CLR 27 2D MLG	LCE
M29004	COMM CO CLR 37 3D MLG	LCE
M29053	COMM CO H&S BN 4TH MLG	LCE
P28303	COMM CO HQTRS REGT 1ST MLG	LCE
M27103	COMM CO HQTRS REGT 2D MLG	LCE
M29004	COMM CO HQTRS REGT 3D MLG	LCE
M20095	MLG FWD (NUCLEUS EAST) H&S BN 4TH MLG	LCE
M20094	MLG FWD (NUCLEUS WEST) H&S BN 4TH MLG	LCE
M75724	DS NBC PLT H&S BN 4TH MLG	LCE

Enclosure (2)

M29054	HQTRS H&S BN 4TH MLG	LCE
M28315	MLG HQTRS 1ST MLG	LCE
M27115	MLG HQTRS 2D MLG	LCE
P27115	MLG HQTRS 2D MLG	LCE
M29017	MLG HQTRS 3D MLG	LCE
M28302	HQTRS CO CLR 17 1ST MLG	LCE
M27102	HQTRS CO CLR 27 2D MLG	LCE
M29002	HQTRS CO CLR 37 3D MLG	LCE
P28302	HQTRS CO HQTRS REGT 1ST MLG	LCE
M27102	HQTRS CO HQTRS REGT 2D MLG	LCE
P29002	HQTRS CO HQTRS REGT 3D MLG	LCE
M28304	SVC CO CLR 17 1ST MLG	LCE
M27108	SVC CO CLR 27 2D MLG	LCE
M29003	SVC CO CLR 37 3D MLG	LCE
M28304	SVC CO HQTRS REGT 1ST MLG	LCE
P27108	SVC CO HQTRS REGT 2D MLG	LCE
M29003	SVC CO HQTRS REGT 3D MLG	LCE
M28308	FD SVC CO CLR 17 1ST MLG	LCE
M27104	FD SVC CO CLR 27 2D MLG	LCE
M29006	FD SVC CO CLR 37 3D MLG	LCE
P28308	FD SVC CO HQTRS REGT 1ST MLG	LCE
M27104	FD SVC CO HQTRS REGT 2D MLG	LCE
M29006	FD SVC CO HQTRS REGT 3D MLG	LCE
M28361	H&S CO CLB 1 CLR 1 1ST MLG	LCE
M27341	H&S CO CLB 2 CLR 2 2D MLG	LCE
M29035	H&S CO CLB 3 CLR 3 3D MLG	LCE
M29031	H&S CO CLB 4 CLR 3 3D MLG	LCE
M28371	H&S CO CLB 5 CLR 1 1ST MLG	LCE
M27351	H&S CO CLB 6 CLR 2 2D MLG	LCE
M28342	H&S CO CLB 7 CLR 1 1ST MLG	LCE
M27361	H&S CO CLB 8 CLR 2 2D MLG	LCE
M28362	SPT CO CLB 1 CLR 1 1ST MLG	LCE
M27342	SPT CO CLB 2 CLR 2 2D MLG	LCE
M29032	SPT CO CLB 4 CLR 3 3D MLG	LCE
M28372	SPT CO CLB 5 CLR 1 1ST MLG	LCE
M27352	SPT CO CLB 6 CLR 2 2D MLG	LCE
M28343	SPT CO CLB 7 CLR 1 1ST MLG	LCE
M27363	SPT CO CLB 8 CLR 2 2D MLG	LCE
M28366	H&S CO CLB 151 CLR 15 1ST MLG	LCE
M28286	H&S CO CLB 153 CLR 15 1ST MLG	LCE
M27366	H&S CO CLB 251 CLR 25 2D MLG	LCE
M27386	H&S CO CLB 253 CLR 25 2D MLG	LCE
M29366	H&S CO CLB 351 CLR 35 3D MLG	LCE
M28332	HQTRS CO CLR 1 1ST MLG	LCE
M27332	HQTRS CO CLR 2 2D MLG	LCE
M29041	HQTRS CO CLR 3 3D MLG	LCE
M28376	HQTRS CO CLR 15 1ST MLG	LCE
M27371	HQTRS CO CLR 25 2D MLG	LCE
M29016	HQTRS CO CLR 35 3D MLG	LCE

Enclosure (2)

M29052	HQTRS CO H&S BN 4TH MLG	LCE
M20195	CLB 11 (11TH MEU) 1ST MLG	LCE
M28391	CLB 13 (13TH MEU) 1ST MLG	LCE
M20196	CLB 15 (15TH MEU) 1ST MLG	LCE
M20197	CLB 22 (22ND MEU) 2D MLG	LCE
M20199	CLB 24 (24TH MEU) 2D MLG	LCE
M20198	CLB 26 (26TH MEU) 2D MLG	LCE
M29048	CLB 31 (31ST MEU) 3D MLG	LCE
M28341	CLC 11 CLR 15 1ST MLG	LCE
M28357	CLC 16 CLR 15 1ST MLG	LCE
M27139	CLC 21 CLR 25 2D MLG	LCE
M27140	CLC 23 CLR 25 2D MLG	LCE
M29049	CLC 36 CLR 35 3D MLG	LCE
M29055	B&T OPS CO A (-) 4TH LSB 4TH MLG	LCE
M29315	B&T OPS CO B (-) 4TH LSB 4TH MLG	LCE
M14551	H&S CO 4TH LSB 4TH MLG	LCE
M29312	DET 1 B&T OPS CO A 4TH LSB 4TH MLG	LCE
M29316	DET 1 B&T OPS CO B 4TH LSB 4TH MLG	LCE
M29313	DET 2 B&T OPS CO A 4TH LSB 4TH MLG	LCE
M29317	DET 2 B&T OPS CO B 4TH LSB 4TH MLG	LCE
M14421	LNDG SPT CO A 4TH LSB 4TH MLG	LCE
M14423	LNDG SPT CO B 4TH LSB 4TH MLG	LCE
M14554	LNDG SPT CO C 4TH LSB 4TH MLG	LCE
M14005	LNDG SPT EQUIP CO 4TH LSB 4TH MLG	LCE
M28336	LNDG SPT CO CLR 17 1ST MLG	LCE
M27335	LNDG SPT CO CLR 27 2D MLG	LCE
M29043	LNDG SPT CO CLR 37 3D MLG	LCE
M28336	LNDG SPT CO HQTRS REGT 1ST MLG	LCE
P27335	LNDG SPT CO HQTRS REGT 2D MLG	LCE
M29043	LNDG SPT CO HQTRS REGT 3D MLG	LCE
M21307	EOD CO 7TH ESB 1ST MLG	LCE
M21316	EOD CO 8TH ESB 2D MLG	LCE
M29106	EOD CO 9TH ESB 3D MLG	LCE
M11021	H&S CO 1ST MED BN 1ST MLG	LCE
M28271	H&S CO 2D MED BN 2D MLG	LCE
M28261	H&S CO 3D MED BN 3D MLG	LCE
M14021	H&S CO 4TH MED BN 4TH MLG	LCE
M11022	SURG CO A 1ST MED BN 1ST MLG	LCE
M28272	SURG CO A 2D MED BN 2D MLG	LCE
M28263	SURG CO A 3D MED BN 3D MLG	LCE
M14022	SURG CO A 4TH MED BN 4TH MLG	LCE
M11023	SURG CO B 1ST MED BN 1ST MLG	LCE
M28273	SURG CO B 2D MED BN 2D MLG	LCE
M28262	SURG CO B 3D MED BN 3D MLG	LCE
M14027	SURG CO B 4TH MED BN 4TH MLG	LCE
M11024	SURG CO C 1ST MED BN 1ST MLG	LCE
M28274	SURG CO C 2D MED BN 2D MLG	LCE
M28263	SURG CO C 3D MED BN CLR 35 3D MLG	LCE
M14673	PERS RET & PROC CO H&S BN 4TH MLG	LCE

M28381	H&S CO 1ST DEN BN 1ST MLG	LCE
M27161	H&S CO 2D DEN BN 2D MLG	LCE
M29091	H&S CO 3D DEN BN 3D MLG	LCE
M29121	H&S CO 4TH DEN BN 4TH MLG	LCE
M29093	11TH DEN CO 3D DEN BN 3D MLG	LCE
M27163	12TH DEN CO 2D DEN BN 2D MLG	LCE
M28383	13TH DEN CO 1ST DEN BN 1ST MLG	LCE
M29123	14TH DEN CO 4TH DEN BN 4TH MLG	LCE
M28382	1ST DEN CO 1ST DEN BN 1ST MLG	LCE
M29094	21ST DEN CO 3D DEN BN 3D MLG	LCE
M27164	22D DEN CO 2D DEN BN 2D MLG	LCE
M28384	23D DEN CO 1ST DEN BN 1ST MLG	LCE
M29124	24TH DEN CO 4TH DEN BN 4TH MLG	LCE
M27162	2D DEN CO 2D DEN BN 2D MLG	LCE
M29092	3D DEN CO 3D DEN BN 3D MLG	LCE
M29122	4TH DEN CO 4TH DEN BN 4TH MLG	LCE
M28367	MAINT CO CLB 151 CLR 15 1ST MLG	LCE
M28287	MAINT CO CLB 153 CLR 15 1ST MLG	LCE
M27367	MAINT CO CLB 251 CLR 25 2D MLG	LCE
M27387	MAINT CO CLB 253 CLR 25 2D MLG	LCE
M29367	MAINT CO CLB 351 CLR 35 3D MLG	LCE
P28362	MAINT SVCS CO CLB 1 CLR 1 1ST MLG	LCE
P27342	MAINT SVCS CO CLB 2 CLR 2 2D MLG	LCE
M29037	MAINT SVCS CO CLB 3 CLR 3 3D MLG	LCE
P29032	MAINT SVCS CO CLB 4 CLR 3 3D MLG	LCE
P28372	MAINT SVCS CO CLB 5 CLR 1 1ST MLG	LCE
P27352	MAINT SVCS CO CLB 6 CLR 2 2D MLG	LCE
P28343	MAINT SVCS CO CLB 7 CLR 1 1ST MLG	LCE
M28322	H&S CO 1ST MAINT BN CLR 15 1ST MLG	LCE
M27122	H&S CO 2D MAINT BN CLR 25 2D MLG	LCE
M29022	H&S CO 3D MAINT BN CLR 35 3D MLG	LCE
M29071	H&S CO 4TH MAINT BN 4TH MLG	LCE
M28324	ELMACO 1ST MAINT BN CLR 15 1ST MLG	LCE
M27124	ELMACO 2D MAINT BN CLR 25 2D MLG	LCE
M29025	ELMACO 3D MAINT BN CLR 35 3D MLG	LCE
M29072	ELMACO 4TH MAINT BN 4TH MLG	LCE
M28325	ENGR MAINT CO 1ST MAINT BN CLR 15 1ST MLG	LCE
M27131	ENGR MAINT CO 2D MAINT BN CLR 25 2D MLG	LCE
M29024	ENGR MAINT CO 3D MAINT BN CLR 35 3D MLG	LCE
M29074	ENGR MAINT CO 4TH MAINT BN 4TH MLG	LCE
M28327	ORD MAINT CO 1ST MAINT BN CLR 15 1ST MLG	LCE
M27127	ORD MAINT CO 2D MAINT BN CLR 25 2D MLG	LCE
M29023	ORD MAINT CO 3D MAINT BN CLR 35 3D MLG	LCE
M74746	ORD MAINT CO 4TH MAINT BN 4TH MLG	LCE
M28326	MTM CO 1ST MAINT BN CLR 15 1ST MLG	LCE
M27132	MTM CO 2D MAINT BN CLR 25 2D MLG	LCE
M29026	MTM CO 3D MAINT BN CLR 35 3D MLG	LCE
M29075	MTM CO 4TH MAINT BN 4TH MLG	LCE
M28328	GSM CO 1ST MAINT BN CLR 15 1ST MLG	LCE

Enclosure (2)

M27128	GSM CO 2D MAINT BN CLR 25 2D MLG	LCE
M29027	GSM CO 3D MAINT BN CLR 35 3D MLG	LCE
M29076	GSM CO 4TH MAINT BN 4TH MLG	LCE
M28358	GS MAINT CO CLR 15 1ST MLG	LCE
M27146	GS MAINT CO CLR 25 2D MLG	LCE
M29364	GS MAINT CO CLR 35 3D MLG	LCE
M28311	H&S CO 1ST SUP BN CLR 15 1ST MLG	LCE
M27118	H&S CO 2D SUP BN CLR 25 2D MLG	LCE
M29011	H&S CO 3D SUP BN CLR 35 3D MLG	LCE
M29061	H&S CO 4TH SUP BN 4TH MLG	LCE
M29064	RATIONS CO 4TH SUP BN 4TH MLG	LCE
M28313	AMMO CO 1ST SUP BN CLR 15 1ST MLG	LCE
M27113	AMMO CO 2D SUP BN CLR 25 2D MLG	LCE
M29013	AMMO CO 3D SUP BN CLR 35 3D MLG	LCE
M73757	AMMO CO 4TH SUP BN 4TH MLG	LCE
M77006	GS AMMO PLT AMMO CO 4TH SUP BN 4TH MLG	LCE
M28312	SUP CO 1ST SUP BN CLR 15 1ST MLG	LCE
M27119	SUP CO 2D SUP BN CLR 25 2D MLG	LCE
M29012	SUP CO 3D SUP BN CLR 35 3D MLG	LCE
M29065	SUP CO 4TH SUP BN 4TH MLG	LCE
M28368	SUP CO CLB 151 CLR 15 1ST MLG	LCE
M28288	SUP CO CLB 153 CLR 15 1ST MLG	LCE
M27368	SUP CO CLB 251 CLR 25 2D MLG	LCE
M27388	SUP CO CLB 253 CLR 25 2D MLG	LCE
M29368	SUP CO CLB 351 CLR 35 3D MLG	LCE
M28333	MEDLOG CO 1ST SUP BN CLR 15 1ST MLG	LCE
M27117	MEDLOG CO 2D SUP BN CLR 25 2D MLG	LCE
M29014	MEDLOG CO 3D SUP BN CLR 35 3D MLG	LCE
M29066	MEDLOG CO 4TH SUP BN 4TH MLG	LCE
M71776	MP CO A H&S BN 4TH MLG	LCE
M14235	MP CO B H&S BN 4TH MLG	LCE
M71778	MP CO C H&S BN 4TH MLG	LCE
M28111	H&S CO 6TH MT BN 4TH MLG	LCE
M28337	GS MT CO CLR 1 1ST MLG	LCE
M27336	GS MT CO CLR 2 2D MLG	LCE
M29042	GS MT CO CLR 3 3D MLG	LCE
M28338	MT CO CLB 1 CLR 1 1ST MLG	LCE
M27337	MT CO CLB 2 CLR 2 2D MLG	LCE
M29044	MT CO CLB 4 CLR 3 3D MLG	LCE
M28339	MT CO CLB 5 CLR 1 1ST MLG	LCE
M27338	MT CO CLB 6 CLR 2 2D MLG	LCE
M28346	MT CO CLB 7 CLR 1 1ST MLG	LCE
M27362	MT CO CLB 8 CLR 2 2D MLG	LCE
P28338	TRANS SVCS CO CLB 1 CLR 1 1ST MLG	LCE
P27337	TRANS SVCS CO CLB 2 CLR 2 2D MLG	LCE
M29036	TRANS SVCS CO CLB 3 CLR 3 3D MLG	LCE
P29044	TRANS SVCS CO CLB 4 CLR 3 3D MLG	LCE
P28339	TRANS SVCS CO CLB 5 CLR 1 1ST MLG	LCE
P27338	TRANS SVCS CO CLB 6 CLR 2 2D MLG	LCE

Enclosure (2)

P28346	TRANS SVCS CO CLB 7 CLR 1 1ST MLG	LCE
M28369	MT CO CLB 151 CLR 15 1ST MLG	LCE
M28289	MT CO CLB 153 CLR 15 1ST MLG	LCE
M27369	MT CO CLB 251 CLR 25 2D MLG	LCE
M27389	MT CO CLB 253 CLR 25 2D MLG	LCE
M29369	MT CO CLB 351 CLR 35 3D MLG	LCE
M28115	GS MT CO 6TH MT BN 4TH MLG	LCE
M14654	DS MT CO A (-) 6TH MT BN 4TH MLG	LCE
M14652	DS MT CO B (-) 6TH MT BN 4TH MLG	LCE
M28213	DET DS MT CO A 6TH MT BN 4TH MLG	LCE
M28214	DET DS MT CO B 6TH MT BN 4TH MLG	LCE
M83190	SITE SPT (ALBANY GA) 4TH SUP BN 4TH MLG	LCE
M81236	SITE SPT (ALLENTOWN) 4TH MAINT BN 4TH MLG	LCE
M83170	SITE SPT (AUGUSTA) 4TH MAINT BN 4TH MLG	LCE
M87281	SITE SPT (BAKERSFIELD) 6TH ESB 4TH MLG	LCE
M85236	SITE SPT (BATTLE CREEK) 6TH ESB 4TH MLG	LCE
M83181	SITE SPT (CAMP LEJEUNE) 4TH LSB 4TH MLG	LCE
M83227	SITE SPT (CHARLESTON) 4TH LSB 4TH MLG	LCE
M83268	SITE SPT (CHARLOTTE) 4TH MAINT BN 4TH MLG	LCE
M87227	SITE SPT (CONCORD) 4TH LSB 4TH MLG	LCE
M81247	SITE SPT (DAYTON) H&S BN 4TH MLG	LCE
M84261	SITE SPT (DYESS AFB) 4TH MAINT BN 4TH MLG	LCE
M87244	SITE SPT (EUGENE) 6TH ESB 4TH MLG	LCE
M81229	SITE SPT (FOLSOM) 6TH ESB 4TH MLG	LCE
M80172	SITE SPT (FT DEVENS) 4TH MAINT BN 4TH MLG	LCE
M87229	SITE SPT (FT LEWIS) 4TH LSB 4TH MLG	LCE
M85219	SITE SPT (FT WAYNE) H&S BN 4TH MLG	LCE
M87269	SITE SPT (GREEN BAY) 6TH ESB 4TH MLG	LCE
M29301	SITE SPT (GREENSBORO) H&S BN 4TH MLG	LCE
M83302	SITE SPT (GREENVILLE) 4TH SUP BN 4TH MLG	LCE
M87226	SITE SPT (LATHROP) 4TH LSB 4TH MLG	LCE
M81238	SITE SPT (LEXINGTON) H&S BN 4TH MLG	LCE
M84258	SITE SPT (LUBBOCK) 6TH MT BN 4TH MLG	LCE
M83304	SITE SPT (MARIETTA) 4TH SUP BN 4TH MLG	LCE
M29300	SITE SPT (MARIETTA) H&S BN 4TH MLG	LCE
M80296	SITE SPT (NEW HAVEN) 6TH MT BN 4TH MLG	LCE
M82266	SITE SPT (NEWPORT NEWS) 4TH SUP BN 4TH MLG	LCE
M80297	SITE SPT (NEWPORT) 6TH MT BN 4TH MLG	LCE
M85245	SITE SPT (OMAHA) 4TH MAINT BN 4TH MLG	LCE
M83231	SITE SPT (ORLANDO) 6TH MT BN 4TH MLG	LCE
M85234	SITE SPT (PEORIA) 6TH ESB 4TH MLG	LCE
M87243	SITE SPT (PHOENIX) 6TH ESB 4TH MLG	LCE
M81239	SITE SPT (PITTSBURGH) H&S BN 4TH MLG	LCE
M87241	SITE SPT (PORTLAND) 6TH ESB 4TH MLG	LCE
M80297	SITE SPT (PROVIDENCE) 6TH MT BN 4TH MLG	LCE
M83300	SITE SPT (RALEIGH) 4TH SUP BN 4TH MLG	LCE
M80295	SITE SPT (RED BANK) 6TH MT BN 4TH MLG	LCE
M85249	SITE SPT (ROCK ISLAND) 4TH MAINT BN 4TH MLG	LCE
M83182	SITE SPT (ROOSEVELT RDS) 4TH LSB 4TH MLG	LCE

Enclosure (2)

M87262	SITE SPT (SACRAMENTO) 4TH MAINT BN 4TH MLG	LCE
M87247	SITE SPT (SAN JOSE) 4TH LSB 4TH MLG	LCE
M83180	SITE SPT (SAVANNAH) 4TH LSB 4TH MLG	LCE
M85281	SITE SPT (SOUTH BEND) 6TH ESB 4TH MLG	LCE
M84237	SITE SPT (TEXARKANA) 6TH MT BN 4TH MLG	LCE
M85297	SITE SPT (TOPEKA) 4TH SUP BN 4TH MLG	LCE
M87263	SITE SPT (TUCSON) 6TH ESB 4TH MLG	LCE
M81219	SITE SPT (VIENNA) 4TH LSB 4TH MLG	LCE
M84272	SITE SPT (WACO) 4TH MAINT BN 4TH MLG	LCE
M85248	SITE SPT (WICHITA) 4TH MAINT BN 4TH MLG	LCE
M81235	SITE SPT (WILMINGTON) 6TH ESB 4TH MLG	LCE
M75731	DET 1 COMM CO H&S BN 4TH MLG	LCE
M29077	DET 1 ELMACO 4TH MAINT BN 4TH MLG	LCE
M22304	DET 1 ENGR SPT CO 6TH ESB 4TH MLG	LCE
M28209	DET 1 GS MT CO 6TH MT BN 4TH MLG	LCE
M29224	DET 1 H&S CO 4TH LSB 4TH MLG	LCE
M22301	DET 1 H&S CO 6TH ESB 4TH MLG	LCE
M28201	DET 1 H&S CO 6TH MT BN 4TH MLG	LCE
M29205	DET 1 HQTRS CO H&S BN 4TH MLG	LCE
M29303	DET 1 LNDG SPT EQUIP CO 4TH LSB 4TH MLG	LCE
M74860	DET 1 MTM CO 4TH MAINT BN 4TH MLG	LCE
M14663	DET 1 SUP CO 4TH SUP BN 4TH MLG	LCE
M22313	DET 10 ENGR SPT CO 6TH ESB 4TH MLG	LCE
M29214	DET 10 HQTRS CO H&S BN 4TH MLG	LCE
M22314	DET 11 ENGR SPT CO 6TH ESB 4TH MLG	LCE
M71007	DET 2 COMM CO H&S BN 4TH MLG	LCE
M29078	DET 2 ELMACO 4TH MAINT BN 4TH MLG	LCE
M22305	DET 2 ENGR SPT CO 6TH ESB 4TH MLG	LCE
M28210	DET 2 GS MT CO 6TH MT BN 4TH MLG	LCE
M29225	DET 2 H&S CO 4TH LSB 4TH MLG	LCE
M22302	DET 2 H&S CO 6TH ESB 4TH MLG	LCE
M28202	DET 2 H&S CO 6TH MT BN 4TH MLG	LCE
M29206	DET 2 HQTRS CO H&S BN 4TH MLG	LCE
M29304	DET 2 LNDG SPT EQUIP CO 4TH LSB 4TH MLG	LCE
M14664	DET 2 MTM CO 4TH MAINT BN 4TH MLG	LCE
M77004	DET 2 SUP CO 4TH SUP BN 4TH MLG	LCE
M22306	DET 3 ENGR SPT CO 6TH ESB 4TH MLG	LCE
M28211	DET 3 GS MT CO 6TH MT BN 4TH MLG	LCE
M29226	DET 3 H&S CO 4TH LSB 4TH MLG	LCE
M28203	DET 3 H&S CO 6TH MT BN 4TH MLG	LCE
M29207	DET 3 HQTRS CO H&S BN 4TH MLG	LCE
M29305	DET 3 LNDG SPT EQUIP CO 4TH LSB 4TH MLG	LCE
M14666	DET 3 MTM CO 4TH MAINT BN 4TH MLG	LCE
M29068	DET 3 SUP CO 4TH SUP BN 4TH MLG	LCE
M22307	DET 4 ENGR SPT CO 6TH ESB 4TH MLG	LCE
M29227	DET 4 H&S CO 4TH LSB 4TH MLG	LCE
M28204	DET 4 H&S CO 6TH MT BN 4TH MLG	LCE
M29208	DET 4 HQTRS CO H&S BN 4TH MLG	LCE
M29306	DET 4 LNDG SPT EQUIP CO 4TH LSB 4TH MLG	LCE

M22308	DET 5 ENGR SPT CO 6TH ESB 4TH MLG	LCE
M29228	DET 5 H&S CO 4TH LSB 4TH MLG	LCE
M28205	DET 5 H&S CO 6TH MT BN 4TH MLG	LCE
M29209	DET 5 HQTRS CO H&S BN 4TH MLG	LCE
M29307	DET 5 LNDG SPT EQUIP CO 4TH LSB 4TH MLG	LCE
M22309	DET 6 ENGR SPT CO 6TH ESB 4TH MLG	LCE
M28206	DET 6 H&S CO 6TH MT BN 4TH MLG	LCE
M29210	DET 6 HQTRS CO H&S BN 4TH MLG	LCE
M29308	DET 6 LNDG SPT EQUIP CO 4TH LSB 4TH MLG	LCE
M22310	DET 7 ENGR SPT CO 6TH ESB 4TH MLG	LCE
M29211	DET 7 HQTRS CO H&S BN 4TH MLG	LCE
M29309	DET 7 LNDG SPT EQUIP CO 4TH LSB 4TH MLG	LCE
M22311	DET 8 ENGR SPT CO 6TH ESB 4TH MLG	LCE
M29212	DET 8 HQTRS CO H&S BN 4TH MLG	LCE
M29310	DET 8 LNDG SPT EQUIP CO 4TH LSB 4TH MLG	LCE
M22312	DET 9 ENGR SPT CO 6TH ESB 4TH MLG	LCE
M29213	DET 9 HQTRS CO H&S BN 4TH MLG	LCE
M77060	DET AMMO CO 4TH SUP BN 4TH MLG	LCE
M29921	DET ENGR MAINT CO 4TH MAINT BN 4TH MLG	LCE
M14023	DET H&S CO 4TH MED BN 4TH MLG	LCE
M21682	DET HQTRS CO 6TH COMM BN 4TH MLG	LCE
M29067	DET MEDLOG CO 4TH SUP BN 4TH MLG	LCE
M70694	DET ORD MAINT CO 4TH MAINT BN 4TH MLG	LCE
M14674	DET PERS RET & PROC CO H&S BN 4TH MLG	LCE
M14026	DET SURG CO A 4TH MED BN 4TH MLG	LCE
M14024	DET SURG CO B 4TH MED BN 4TH MLG	LCE
M21687	DET SVC CO 6TH COMM BN 4TH MLG	LCE
M53502	MCESG HQTRS	SE
M53503	MCESG REGION 1	SE
M53504	MCESG REGION 2	SE
M53505	MCESG REGION 3	SE
M53506	MCESG REGION 4	SE
M53509	MCESG REGION 5	SE
M53508	MCESG REGION 6	SE
M53510	MCESG REGION 7	SE
M53511	MCESG REGION 8	SE
M53507	MCESG REGION 9	SE

Priority Commands

UIC	UNIT NAME	MAGTF
MS0345	FASOTRAGRU MCAS MIRAMAR CA	ACE
MS5117	USN FLT DEMO TM NAS PENSACOLA FL	ACE
MS0347	DET CNATTU LITTLE ROCK AR	ACE
M32004	1ST RECRUIT TRNG BN RTR MCRD PISC	SE
M10204	1ST RECRUIT TRNG BN RTR MCRD SDCA	SE
M32005	2D RECRUIT TRNG BN RTR MCRD PISC	SE
M10205	2D RECRUIT TRNG BN RTR MCRD SDCA	SE
M32006	3D RECRUIT TRNG BN RTR MCRD PISC	SE
M10206	3D RECRUIT TRNG BN RTR MCRD SDCA	SE
M32008	4TH RECRUIT TRNG BN RTR MCRD PISC	SE
MS5106	ADMIN AND RES MGMNT (A&R) DIV HQMC	SE
M31040	ADV INF TRNG BN SOI EAST TRNG COM	SE
M33040	ADV INF TRNG BN SOI WEST TRNG COM	SE
MS3800	ASLT AMPHIB BN SCOL BN TRNG COM MCB CAMPEN CA	SE
MS5109	CMD CTRL COMM & COMP DEPT (C4) HQMC	SE
MS5802	CO A MARINE CRYPTO SPT BN MCIA	SE
MS5803	CO B MARINE CRYPTO SPT BN MCIA	SE
MS5804	CO D MARINE CRYPTO SPT BN MCIA	SE
MS5805	CO G MARINE CRYPTO SPT BN MCIA	SE
MS5806	CO H MARINE CRYPTO SPT BN MCIA	SE
MS5807	CO I MARINE CRYPTO SPT BN MCIA	SE
MS5808	CO L MARINE CRYPTO SPT BN MCIA	SE
MS5116	DC AVIATION (AVN) DEPT HQMC	SE
MS5112	DC INSTAL & LOGISTICS (I&L) DEPT HQMC	SE
MS5102	DC MPR AND RES AFFAIRS (M&RA) DEPT HQMC	SE
MS5114	DC PLANS POLICIES & OPS (PP&O) DEPT HQMC	SE
MS5113	DC PROG & RES (P&R) DEPT HQMC	SE
MS4209	DEF ADV RESEARCH PROJ AGENCY (DARPA)	SE
MS4144	DEF CNTRCT MGMNT AGENCY (DCMA)	SE
MS3219	DEF EQUAL OPP MGMT INST TRNG COM PATRICK AFB FL	SE
MS4214	DEF FIN & ACCT SERVICE (DFAS) CLEVELAND OH	SE
MS4104	DEF INFO SYSTEMS AGENCY (DISA)	SE
MS4113	DEF INTEL AGENCY (DIA)	SE
MS4206	DEF LEGAL SERV AGENCY	SE
MS4147	DEF MEDIA ACT	SE
MS3212	DEF NUC WPNS SCOL TRNG COM KIRTLAND AFB NM	SE
MS4211	DEF THREAT REDUCTION AGENCY	SE
MS5129	DET CMBT CARGO/ ASST AIR OPS	SE
MS4200	DOD ACTIVITIES MISC	SE
MS5507	DRUM & BUGLE CORPS MARBKS WASH DC	SE
MS5980	EXPED WARFARE TRNG GRP (EWTG) LANT	SE
MS7271	EXPED WARFARE TRNG GRP (EWTG) PAC	SE
MS5133	EXPEDITIONARY STRIKE GROUPS	SE
MS3207	FIN MGMT SCOL MCCSSS TRNG COM CAMLEJ NC	SE
MS3089	FLD MED TRNG BN EAST	SE
MS3950	FLD MED TRNG BN WEST	SE

MS5128	FLG & STF ALLOW US LANT/ NAVEUR	SE
MS5130	FLG & STF ALLOW US PAC/ NAVCENT	SE
MS3204	GRD SUPP SCOL MCCSSS TRNG COM CAMLEJ NC	SE
MS5509	GUARD CO MARBKS WASH DC	SE
M32001	H&S BN MCRD PISC	SE
M10201	H&S BN MCRD SDCA	SE
MS5501	H&S CO MARINE BARRACKS WASH DC	SE
MS5101	HQMC SEPARATE OFFICES	SE
M31050	HQTRS AND SPT BN SOI EAST TRNG COM	SE
M33050	HQTRS AND SPT BN SOI WEST TRNG COM	SE
MS4105	HQTRS DEF LOGISTICS AGENCY	SE
M30071	HQTRS MARCOR INTEL SCOLS (MCIS) TRNG COM DAM NECK	SE
MS5601	HQTRS MARINE CORPS RECRUITING COM	SE
MS5801	HQTRS MARINE CRYPTO SPT BN MCIA	SE
M32003	HQTRS RTR MCRD PISC	SE
M10203	HQTRS RTR MCRD SDCA	SE
MS4108	HQTRS US SPEC OPS COM (USSOCOM)	SE
M31030	INF TRNG BN SOI EAST TRNG COM	SE
M33030	INF TRNG BN SOI WEST TRNG COM	SE
MS5126	INSP GEN OF THE MARINE CORPS	SE
MS5121	INTELLIGENCE (INTEL) DEPT HQMC	SE
MS4107	INTL MIL ACT NATO	SE
MS4148	JIAMDO	SE
MS4126	JT CTR FOR INTERNATIONAL SECURITY FORCE ASSISTANCE	SE
MS3213	JT FIREPWR CNTL COURSE TRNG COM NELLIS AFB NV	SE
MS5115	JUDGE ADVOCATE (JA) DIV HQMC	SE
MS3205	LOG OPS SCOL MCCSSS TRNG COM CAMLEJ NC	SE
MS4102	MARCOR ASGN TO THE JOINT STAFF	SE
MS3236	MARCOR DET DEF LANG INST TRNG COM MONTEREY CA	SE
MS3279	MARCOR DET FLEET TRNG CTR TRNG COM NORFOLK VA	SE
MS3232	MARCOR DET FT LVNWRTH KS	SE
MS3270	MARCOR DET TRNG COM DAM NECK	SE
MS3256	MARCOR DET TRNG COM FORT MEADE MD	SE
MS3281	MARCOR DET TRNG COM FT BELVOIR VA	SE
M67700	MARCOR DET TRNG COM FT LEONARD WOOD	SE
MS3220	MARCOR DET TRNG COM GOODFELLOW AFB TX	SE
MS3221	MARCOR DET TRNG COM KEESLER AFB MS	SE
MS3215	MARCOR DET TRNG COM LACKLAND AFB TX	SE
MS3264	MARCOR DET TRNG COM NAS CORRY STATION FL	SE
MS3275	MARCOR DET TRNG COM NEWPORT RI	SE
MS3248	MARCOR DET USA AIR DEF SCOL TRNG COM FT BLISS TX	SE
MS3247	MARCOR DET USA ARTY CTR TRNG COM FT SILL OK	SE
MS3231	MARCOR DET USA CMD STAFF COL EDU COM FT LVNWRTH KS	SE
MS3234	MARCOR DET USA INTEL SCOL TRNG COM FT HUACHUCA AZ	SE
MS3252	MARCOR DET USA SIGNAL SCOL TRNG COM FT GORDON GA	SE
MS3276	MARCOR DET USN WARFARE DEV COM TRG COM NORFOLK VA	SE
MS3267	MARCOR DET USN CHAPLAINS SCOL TRNG COM NEWPORT RI	SE
MS5107	MARCOR INSTR STAFF NROTC	SE

Enclosure (3)

MS3277	MARCOR LSN ADV ELEC DIV SCOL TRNG COM SAN DIEGO CA	SE
MS3216	MARCOR LSN CBL SPLICER INST CRS TRNG COM SHPD AFB	SE
MS3265	MARCOR LSN USN DIVG SALV CTR TRNG COM PANAMA CT FL	SE
MS5108	MARCOR PERS ASGN SERVICE ACADS	SE
MS3211	MARCOR REP AIR UNIV EDU COM MAXWELL AFB	SE
MS3237	MARCOR REP DEF ACQUIS UNIV TRNG COM FT BELVOIR	SE
MS3238	MARCOR REP DEF MAP SCOL TRNG COM FT BELVOIR VA	SE
MS3291	MARCOR REP NATL DEF UNIV (NDU) EDU COM	SE
MS3280	MARCOR REP NAV SML CRF INSTR SCOL TRNG COM STNS MS	SE
MS3271	MARCOR REP NVL SCOL MUSIC TRNG COM NAB LTL CRK VA	SE
MS3273	MARCOR REP SERE TRNG COM NAS N ISL SAN DIEGO CA	SE
MS3274	MARCOR REP SERE-E TRNG CMD NAVSHIPYD PORTSMOUTH	SE
MS3245	MARCOR REP TRNG COM FT JACKSON SC	SE
MS3262	MARCOR REP US NAVAL POST GRADUATE SCHOOL TRNG COM	SE
MS3261	MARCOR REP US NAVAL WAR COLL EDU COM NEWPORT RI	SE
MS3263	MARCOR REP US NAVAL WAR COLL EDU COM NEWPORT RI	SE
MS3241	MARCOR REP USA INFANTRY SCOL TRNG COM FT BENNING	SE
MS3251	MARCOR REP USA JAG SCOL TRNG COM CHARLOTTESVLE VA	SE
MS3246	MARCOR REP USA SPEC OPS COM CTR TRNG COM FT BRG NC	SE
MS3250	MARCOR REP USA TRANS SCOL TRNG COM FT EUSTIS VA	SE
MS3233	MARCOR REP USA WAR COLLEGE EDU COM CARLISE PA	SE
MS3218	MARCOR REP USAF AIR/GND OPS TRNG COM HLBRT FLD FL	SE
MS3257	MARCORDET USA MFF SCOL YUMA PROVIN GDS YUMA AZ	SE
MS3214	MARDET NAVSCOL EOD TRNG COM EGLIN AFB FL	SE
M31020	MARINE CMBT TRNG BN SOI EAST TRNG COM	SE
M33020	MARINE CMBT TRNG BN SOI WEST TRNG COM	SE
MS4121	MARINE CORPS ASSIGNED ALLIED/UN COMMANDS	SE
MS4204	MARINE CORPS PERS DON NON-DEPT	SE
M06050	MATSG-21 TRNG COM NAS PENSACOLA FL	SE
MS0337	MATSG-22 TRNG COM NAS CORPUS CHRISTI TX	SE
MS0336	MATSG-23 TRNG COM NAS LEMOORE CA	SE
MS0339	MATSG-33 TRNG COM NAS OCEANA VA	SE
MS0335	MATSG-53 TRNG COM NAS WHIDBEY ISL WA	SE
MS0346	MATSS-1 NAS MERIDIAN MS	SE
MS4212	MC PERS ASSIGNED TO USA/USAF	SE
M30000	MCCDC	SE
MS5111	MCNOSC	SE
MS4210	MILITARY POSTAL SERVICE AGENCY	SE
MS4208	MISSILE DEFENSE AGENCY	SE
M33060	MOB TRNG BN SOI WEST TRNG COM	SE
MS4143	NATL AERO AND SPACE ADMIN (NASA)	SE
MS4205	NATIONAL GEOSPARTIAL INTEL AGENCY	SE
MS5131	NON-LETHAL WPNS DIR	SE
M30380	OCS TRNG COM QUANTICO VA	SE
MS4103	OFFICE OF THE SECNAV	SE
MS4101	OSD JOINT BILLETS	SE
MS4109	OSD JOINT CRITICAL BILLETS	SE
MS4123	OSD MOBILIZATION BILLETS	SE

MS4122	OSD NON JOINT BILLETS	SE
MS4207	PENTAGON FORCE PROTECTION AGENCY	SE
MS3224	PERS ADMIN SCOL MCCSSS TRNG COM CAMLEJ NC	SE
MS5105	PERSONNEL FAMILY RED DIV	SE
MS5104	PERSONNEL MANAGEMENT DIV MM	SE
MS5123	PUBLIC AFFAIRS (PA) DIV HQMC	SE
MS5103	RESERVE AFFAIRS (RA) DIV HQMC	SE
MS5502	RFL CO A MARBKS WASH DC	SE
MS5503	RFL CO B MARBKS WASH DC	SE
MS5125	SAFETY DIVISION HQMC	SE
M93260	SCOL OF INF (SOI) TRNG COM MCB CAMLEJ NC	SE
M93250	SCOL OF INF (SOI) TRNG COM MCB CAMPEN CA	SE
M93059	SNCO ACAD EDU COM CAMLEJ NC	SE
MS3030	SNCO ACAD EDU COM QUANTICO VA	SE
M20240	SNCOA EDU COM CAMP BUTLER JA	SE
MS3310	SNCOA EDU COM CAMPEN CA	SE
MS3308	SNCOA SGTS CRS EDU COM 29 PALMS CA	SE
MS3311	SNCOA SGTS CRS EDU COM MCB KANEOHE HI	SE
MS4213	SPECIAL REQUIREMENTS T/O	SE
M32009	SPT BN RTR MCRD PISC	SE
M10209	SPT BN RTR MCRD SDCA	SE
M30300	TBS TRNG COM QUANTICO VA	SE
MS4127	US AFRICA COMMAND (AFRICOM)	SE
MS4111	US CENTCOM (USCENTCOM)	SE
MS4115	US EUROPEAN COMMAND (USEUCOM)	SE
MS4110	US JT FOR COM (USJFCOM)	SE
MS3305	US MARCOR COMM SCOL TRNG COM QUANTICO VA	SE
MS5505	US MARINE CORPS BAND WASH DC	SE
MS4117	US NORTHERN COMMAND (USNORTHCOM)	SE
MS4112	US PACIFIC COMMAND (USPACOM)	SE
MS4118	US SOUTHERN COMMAND (USSOUTHCOM)	SE
MS4114	US STRAT COM (USSTRATCOM)	SE
MS4119	US TRANS COM (USTRANSCOM)	SE
MS3053	USMC CMBT SVC SPT SCOLS MCCSSS TRN COM CAMLEJ NC	SE
MS3303	USMC COM & STAFF COLL EDU COM QUANTICO VA	SE
M35200	USMC COMM ELEC SCOL TRNG COM 29 PALMS CA	SE
MS3050	USMC ENGR SCOL TRNG COM CAMLEJ NC	SE
MS3304	USMC EXP WARFARE SCOL EDU COM QUANTICO VA	SE
MS4106	WHITE HOUSE JOINT BILLET	SE
M32007	WPNS & FLD TRNG BN MCRD PISC	SE
M10207	WPNS & FLD TRNG BN MCRD SDCA	SE
M38600	MTN WARFARE TRNG CNTR TRNG COM BRIDGEPORT CA	SE
MS3512	MAGTF TACT TRNG EXER CTRL GRP TRNG COM 29 PALMS CA	SE
MS3515	ADVISOR TRNG GRP (ATG) MAGTFTC TRNG COM	SE
M30082	CO A MARCOR DET USA QMC & SCOL TRNG COM FT LEE	SE
M30083	CO B MARCOR DET USA QMC & SCOL TRNG COM FT LEE	SE
MS3000	DC CD&I QUANTICO VA	SE
MS4146	DPRI REQUIREMENTS	SE

MS3513	EXERCISE SPT DIV MAGTFTC TRNG COM 29 PALMS CA	SE
M55173	HMX-1 MCAF QUANTICO VA	SE
M30081	HQTRS MARCOR DET USA QMC & SCOL TRNG COM FT LEE	SE
MS4142	JT IMP EXPL DEV DEF ORG (JIEDDO)	SE
MS4640	MARCOR DET NAVEODTECHDIV INDIAN HEAD	SE
M35211	MARCOR LOG OPS GRP 29 PALMS	SE
M30016	MARINE COMBAT TACTICS AND OPS GRP (MCTOG)	SE
MS3001	NCR COMPT AND REGL CONT QUANTICO VA	SE
M54205	OMFR HQMC	SE
M30063	WOUNDED WARRIOR BATTALION (EAST)	SE
M30062	WOUNDED WARRIOR BATTALION (WEST)	SE
M30061	WOUNDED WARRIOR REGIMENT HQ	SE

Proportionate Share Commands

UIC	UNIT NAME	MAGTF
MS5120	DET MARINE AVIATION NAS PATUXENT RIVER MD	ACE
MS5119	DET MARINE AVIATION NWS CHINA LAKE CA	ACE
M02220	VMR-1 MCAS CHERRY POINT NC	ACE
M20018	HQTRS CO HQTRS BN MARFORRES	CE
M20016	HQTRS MARFORRES	CE
MS3324	21 AREA COORD OFF MCB CAMPEN CA	SE
M67500	BLOUNT ISLAND COM	SE
M20810	CAMP MUJUK ROK	SE
M20229	CATC CAMP FUJI JAPAN	SE
MS0343	DET NAVAIRSYSCOM PMA (F)-226 NAS PATUXENT RIVER MD	SE
M93056	DPLMNT PROCESS CMD RSU EAST	SE
MS4306	FRC EAST MCAS CHERRY POINT NC	SE
M67420	GUAM BASE SUPPORT (ADVANCE)	SE
M67353	H&S BN HQMC HENDERSON HALL	SE
M30007	H&S BN MCB QUANTICO VA	SE
M31001	HQTRS AND SPT BN MCB CAMLEJ NC	SE
M33001	HQTRS AND SPT BN MCB CAMPEN CA	SE
M67400	HQTRS MCB CAMP BUTLER JA	SE
M30004	HQTRS MCB QUANTICO VA	SE
MS3015	MAGTF STAFF TRNG PROG (MSTP) TRNG & EDUC COM	SE
MS3510	MAGTF TRNG COM TRNG COM 29 PALMS CA	SE
MS4120	MARCOR FIELD SERVICE ASGN	SE
M30110	MARCOR INFO TECH CNTR KANSAS CITY MO	SE
M67551	MARCOR SPT FAC BLOUNT ISLAND	SE
MS3302	MARCOR UNIV EDU COM TRNG & EDUC COM QUANTICO VA	SE
M38001	MARCORLOGCOM ALBANY GA	SE
M37101	MARCORSYSCOM QUANTICO VA	SE
MS5122	MARINE CORPS INTEL ACT	SE
M38002	MARINE DEPOT MAINTENANCE COMMAND (MDMC)	SE
MS4203	MC OPER TEST/EVAL ACT (MCOTEA)	SE
MS3002	MC WAR FIGHTING LAB (MCWL) QUANTICO VA	SE
M00262	MCAF QUANTICO VA	SE
M02205	MCAS BEAUFORT SC	SE
M02208	MCAS CAMPEN CA	SE
M02207	MCAS CHERRY POINT NC	SE
M02204	MCAS FUTENMA JA	SE
M02203	MCAS IWAKUNI JA	SE
M02211	MCAS KANEOHE BAY HI	SE
M02209	MCAS MIRAMAR CA	SE
M02206	MCAS NEW RIVER NC	SE
M02212	MCAS YUMA AZ	SE
M00318	MCB KBAY HI	SE
MS5506	MCI CO MARBKS WASH DC	SE
M02215	MCICOM	SE
M02213	MCIEAST	SE

M02216	MCIPAC	SE
M02214	MCIWEST	SE
M38441	MCLB ALBANY GA	SE
M38010	MCLB BARSTOW CA	SE
M92840	MCTSSA CAMPEN CA	SE
MS3322	MOB AND TRNG COM RSU MCB CAMPEN CA	SE
MS5110	NAVY MARINE CORPS INTRANET (NMCI) DET	SE
MS3020	PROGRAM EXECUTIVE OFFICE (PEO)	SE
MS4403	RES SPT UNIT MCAS MIRAMAR CA	SE
MS4501	RESERVE BASE SUPPORT NOLA	SE
MS5504	SCTY CO MARBKS WASH DC	SE
M33002	SECURITY BN MCB CAMPEN CA	SE
M30006	SECURITY BN MCB QUANTICO VA	SE
MS5151	TECH SVCS ORG (TSO) P&R DEPT HQMC	SE
MS3180	TRAIN THE TRAINER SCOL (T3S) TRNG COM	SE
MS3201	TRAINING COMMAND T&E COM QUANTICO VA	SE
M30407	TRNG & EDUC COM	SE
M31002	WPNS TRNG BN MCB CAMLEJ NC	SE
M30903	WPNS TRNG BN TRNG COM QUANTICO VA	SE

Enclosure (4)